KV-354-828

Contents

Blandford Management Series
General editor: Geoffrey J. Athill, MBE, FMS, MIAM, AMBIM

TRAINING
Michael Jinks

FINANCE
Dennis Parkinson

Blandford Management Series

Finance

Dennis Parkinson

BLANDFORD PRESS
Poole   Dorset

First published in the U.K. 1979

Copyright © 1979 Blandford Press Ltd.
Link House, West Street
Poole, Dorset, BH15 1LL

ISBN 0 7137 0957 X (Case)
0 7137 1035 7 (Limp)

British Library Cataloguing Data

Parkinson, Dennis
  Finance. – (Blandford management studies
  series).
  1. Corporations – Finance
  2. Industrial management
  I. Title
  658.1'5   HG4026

Set, printed and bound in Great Britain by
Fakenham Press Limited, Fakenham, Norfolk

PART I Function of the System

Chapter One

What is Finance?

In modern life the role of finance is far reaching. Nearly every action by most of the inhabitants of this planet has a financial implication. Even in the most primitive society as soon as it is agreed that three head of cattle equal one wife, then a medium of exchange is established and whether coinage is eventually used or not, there is a financial relationship.

It is this relationship that enables nation to trade with nation and for today's style of living to progress as it does.

At first this relationship can be wholly descriptive but once figures have been introduced, money established and rates of exchange found between countries, communication becomes much easier. Now by the use of numbers there is a common language, understood by all who are able to read, whether or not they speak with the same tongue.

Within a country, this dependency on and understanding of numbers linked with money extends to all aspects of life.

Bringing in the System

For all this to happen, a system is essential. Provided with a basic system financial communication can be made. The individual variations from the basic are not so important if all understand the system at the centre and without endless legislation a good basic system to deal with financial matters has spread through the world over the centuries.

It is not by any means perfect nor is it standard everywhere but there is enough in common to make it the foremost language across the world. It is this need to communicate at a personal level, at a place of work or between government and government that makes a study of the subject so essential to all.

At each level within a country, finance is used in different ways and influences society according to how and where the impact is felt.

Governments plan the vast sums of money they are to spend and then plan to see how this can be raised from the resources, human and otherwise, that are available. As most governments are responsible to someone for their spending their transactions must be recorded and reported. One slip in their system and the effect is felt through the taxation system by the citizens.

Nowadays with the grouping of nations and the financial help they give to each other the international aspects of finance have grown beyond the wildest of dreams.

The impact and the need to understand financial affairs is not confined to government, it reaches down to the business world – not only in trade to record how much is owed but to shape the future course of the business. Systems must be introduced to show the financial position, to allow the owners of the business to see their progress, for taxes to be paid and not overpaid, and to disclose all the information required by the laws of the society.

What is even more important is to be able to apply the financial aspects not to what has occurred in the past, for that cannot be changed, but to the future. When plans for the enterprise are put into financial terms – into one language, the whole aspect of the business can be seen and unless this language is understood by all in business, to a lesser or greater extent according to their needs, a business cannot reach its full potential and the rewards for working cannot flow.

The All Embracing Term

Speak to most people about finance and they conjure up an image of millions of pounds, dollars or yen being manipulated around the world, while at the other extreme, to talk of 'accounts', 'accounting' or 'accountancy' the picture of a book-keeper in a dingy back office with dusty ledgers is brought to mind.

While it is true these are covered in the financial aspects it is perhaps better to state from the outcome the span of this book and its aims.

At first the underlying ideas which look at the recording of the transactions and the reporting of the state of affairs will be explained. Then they will be applied to both the external aspect and the internal aspect of the enterprise. This will mean obtaining an understanding of the methods and to grasp the limitations which must be present.

With the recording done and the summarized contents presented to the managers and other users the next need is to understand what it means – how to interpret the financial accounts and how to apply the techniques of cost accounting to appreciate the significance of situations in business.

The final stage will be to get to know how the information available can be used to plan the business and how the techniques can be used in business decision making.

The final result, it is hoped, will not be accountants, but people able to understand how the mass of financial information available in business can be used to operate the enterprise successfully and who are able to participate fully in discussions where financial matters are raised.

Chapter Two

Concepts, Conventions and Principles

Although there cannot be a set of rules on how to record and report on transactions applicable throughout the world there has to be some concensus of opinion about the underlying ideas. Without these there could be no exchange of information between traders, governments and other users.

These universally accepted sets of rules are not enshrined in legislation but are to be found written out in texts on accountancy published all over the world. They cannot be dated accurately but have grown with the need to record and communicate.

There are two main divisions known as the concepts and the conventions. The concepts are the basic ideas, the theories on how and why certain categories of transaction should be treated in a particular manner. Once the theories have been established and tested and proved to be acceptable the task of the conventions is to set out the limits of their applications.

The Concepts

The main concepts are discussed below, there are many more and all the time fresh thoughts and ideas are developed as to why transactions are treated in a certain way. As technology moves forward so does the theory of accounting and finance. It is not a dead skill but one which lives, grows and adapts to the changing pattern of life.

The business entity concept
One of the main purposes in recording transactions is to monitor the progress of a business, but if within the mass of data all or some of the private transactions of the owner are included

the result will be distorted. If there is more than one owner, the position becomes even more complicated.

Sometimes when there is only one owner it may appear to be unduly restrictive on the grounds that he owns the whole business so why should he not be able to do what he likes with his own money. This point is agreed but for the sake of control it must be as if the owner lends money to himself, in his business capacity from his private capacity.

This transaction is recorded by showing in the records a liability from the business to the owner and giving it a special name, CAPITAL. Profits, which are due to the owner are added to the capital and should the owner wish to withdraw some money from the business or even to get the business to settle some private bills then this is subtracted from the capital.

To assist with this separation it is essential that separate bank accounts are kept for the owner and for the business.

This concept is taken further with the idea of the limited liability company where the owners each contribute an agreed sum to the business and take their withdrawals of profit as dividends. By law the limited liability company is given the status of a person.

The going concern concept
At the end of a financial period a statement of the worth of the business is prepared and for the sake of convenience this is taken to occur at the close of business on the last day. Any transactions occurring afterwards are put to the following period. It is as if a photograph is taken and the position is frozen for ever.

The problem arises with the valuation of the ASSETS , the possessions of the business. To get the true picture of the company they should be valued at that time and the real value would be the amount they would fetch if they were sold. As this would not represent either the cost to the business or the value of the assets in use, this would be misleading to a person trying to assess the state of affairs.

Obviously, when it is known the business will open as usual on the first day of the following period, to attempt to value the assets on these lines would be time consuming, costly and to no practical purpose. It is far more realistic to presume there is an arbitrary 'cut-off' point and to look at a value in use.

For this to be done it is accepted practice for the person preparing the accounts to presume the business is a going concern, at least into the next financial reporting period, unless information is given to the contrary.

When referring to the financial period the most usual length adopted is one calendar year, although some flexibility is often brought in by permitting a company to complete its year after fifty-two weeks or allow a finish on the same day of the week each year, on say, the first Saturday after 31 December. The financial accounts are prepared on this basis but accounts for control purposes often use a shorter period, for example, one month.

Money concept

Not every event happening in a business can be quantified into money terms. For example, the workforce is unhappy and as a result production is not to the expected level. Although this may be the reason for a loss of sales or for the profit's failure to reach the planned level, no true money value can be placed upon it.

Unless an event can be quantified into money terms there is no place for it in the accounts.

This concept does not preclude the making of estimates to meet a future liability which cannot be calculated precisely at the time the accounts are prepared.

By making sure only quantifiable transactions are included, the reader of the accounts is protected from possible manipulation of the results by nebulous possible losses being brought in and hiding the true facts.

Cost concept

A rule for many years has been that transactions and, in particular, assets should be recorded at their original cost irrespective of whether at a later date they will be revalued or written down to reflect a lower value. In this way a firm base on which to make subsequent calculations can be established.

Whilst inflation is low this concept does not give any distortion when assessing the results but immediately the rate of inflation becomes significant some allowance must be made. This problem will be discussed at a much later part of this book.

In the meantime, it is sufficient to state that whilst the published results will be adjusted for inflation it appears the records used to construct those accounts will continue to observe this time-honoured concept.

Revenue concept

In the effort to produce accounts which reflect an up-to-date picture and as well as the revenues and expenses incurred in the period, the timing of introducing these items is of great importance.

There appears to be a choice, either use the time the payments are made or the time when the legal liability to pay the debt is established.

If the time of payment is chosen, this will be easier to record, but on the other hand it would be almost impossible for a large organization to relate payments to the period to which they belong. To find the profit for the period, it is necessary to relate the sales in the period and the expenses incurred in making those sales.

With customers taking full credit terms and sometimes taking too much, the task would be enormous. Instead the accepted practice is to record the sales as soon as the customer obtains legal title to the product or receives the service, and to enter the expenses as the benefit is received. In most cases this means recording the transaction as soon as the invoice is issued for the sales or received for the expenses.

Accruals concept

Very often when services are involved the expense and sometimes the revenue should be allocated over two periods as everything does not relate to the period under review. When this occurs the charge must be allocated in the most fair manner to the period concerned and the balance held for the next period. Sometimes this allocation is on a proportioned basis or otherwise an obvious split can be carried out.

The situation occurs frequently when an invoice relating to an expense is not received until after the ending of the period, although the whole of the expense was for the period concerned. When this happens the liability to the supplier must be recorded in the subsequent period but the charge is treated as an accrual and added to the total expense in the period under review. Subsequent adjustments are made in the recording medium to ensure that while payment is made to the supplier in the subsquent period the expense is not accounted for twice.

Dual entry concept

One feature of the system of recording information in the records is the provision of an arithmetic check. When all recording was carried out manually this was essential so that at least the statements produced at the conclusion of the process could be said to eliminate a double charge.

It was a concept first published in a treatise by a Venetian merchant in 1492 although it is likely that it was being observed in the Mediterranean trading area for a considerable period prior to this.

The concept has stood the test of time through its simplicity and it is only with the coming of the electronic and the mechanical methods of recording that a change has been made. Even now there is still a check made within the system to make sure all items have been entered correctly as a charge or as a benefit.

The dual entry concept is the basis for double entry bookkeeping and in its simplest terms means that when the transactions are being recorded in the records of a business two aspects must be examined. The giver and the receiver.

To take an example of buying a motor car by a business for cash. The giver was the cash supply of the business and the receiver was the total fleet of motor cars in the business. Taken further, if cash had not been paid right away, the records would show the supplier had given up possession of the car. This is recorded as the acquisition by the business of a liability and there would be an addition to the stock of motor cars.

One very important feature of this concept which causes difficulty in understanding it for the first time, is that it is imperative to view this from the point of view of the business. How the supplier deals with the matter in *his* records must be treated as of no consequence.

Realization concept

Whilst the dual aspect concept is important to the recording function, the realization concept plays an important part when assessing results.

Simply stated it means that profits must not be anticipated. Until such a time as the transaction is completed no prior account can be taken of the profit.

An example will demonstrate the point. A business owns a building which it purchased many years ago for £100,000. It has no intention of selling it for another five years but has had it valued and finds it is worth, at present, £500,000. It must not treat the increase in value as profit and distribute it to the owners. It is a potential profit which does not become real, or actual, until the building is sold. It could be that between the time the valuation was made and the sale, the market for factories would have collapsed and only £250,000 would be received. If the paper profit had been distributed to the owners the business would probably have only a slight chance of survival.

Once this concept was taken to the extreme with profits being taken only when a contract was completed. In long-term contracts, such as are found in the construction or the shipbuilding industries, this practice gave a greater distortion than the anticipation of the profit earned to date and the hope that it would not be subsequently lost.

The current practice is to take only a proportion of the profit considered to have been earned in the financial period under review and to make sure all expenses are included.

The Conventions

With the concepts agreed there needs to be some guidance as to how they should be put into use and how far they should go, otherwise there would be excesses, general confusion and finally a disregard for all of them.

The guidance on methods to be used is grouped under what are called the conventions and a selection of them are given.

Convention of objectivity

This convention is clear and simply states that, when presenting reports constructed from financial information, the information presented should be based on the facts arising from the records of transactions and must not reflect the opinion of the author of the reports.

Following this convention does not preclude the presentation of forecasts, as these are to be based on facts. It may be that there has to be some degree of subjectivity but this should be a projection from what has been established.

It must be remembered that financial reports are not a substitute for decision-making. Decisions are still made by human beings in business and no amount of information poured out from even the latest computer will take over. Decisions may be based on the information presented but are not contained within it.

Convention of materiality

In a desire to achieve extreme accuracy the bookkeepers tend to record the facts in extreme detail, often with the professed intention to be ready should the information be required in the future. In turn when the reports reflecting this information are presented they are likely to show this same tendency, often giving a great deal of irrelevant fact.

Two points should be remembered and both are concerned with costs. The first is that the operating of all recording systems costs money and it is foolhardy to waste it on worthless recording of detail. A second point is that reports are presented to executives, in the main, and it is a waste of their valuable time if they have to plough through a mass of items which neither concern them nor are of use to them. Time is money.

The type of detail referred to can be illustrated by the recording of wear on a carpet in the foyer of a large busy hotel. It has been decided to link the depreciation of the carpet to usage and a trip meter has been installed to show how many feet cross the front entrance on to the carpet each day. This fact is duly entered in the records with an appropriate value. The cost of recording is probably more than the cost saved by having this information.

A golden rule is that information should be presented in such detail as is necessary for the making of decisions and no more.

Of course, this convention is not meant to detract from the need for accuracy in recording. Certain items, especially where cash or liabilities are involved, must be recorded to the last penny.

Convention of prudence

This convention used to be known as 'conservatism' and has probably done more to tarnish the reputation of the accountant than anything else.

Not only is it wrong to anticipate profit but when presenting information all possible costs should be included so as to give a pessimistic view rather than taking the over-optimistic outlook.

It is a stricture given to accountants from the very commencement of their training and for a good reason. It is considered to be more desirable to mislead a person slightly by showing things to be worse than they are than to allow decisions to be made with far-reaching and possibly disastrous consequences based on an over-optimistic assessment.

Convention of consistency

In all recording of information or in the presentation of results there should be consistency; any item should be dealt with in the same manner every time.

This does not mean there should never be any change, whether brought about by a more efficient method or otherwise. Should there be a change then it must not be indiscriminate, it must not be followed by a further change or a reversion to the first method, and if the change is in the presentation of results the attention of the user should be drawn to the variation. If comparative figures from a previous period are used they should be altered, if possible, to come into line with the revised method.

13

Convention of stability of currency

Until recently this convention was the mainstay of both the bookkeeper and the presenter of financial reports. Only the historical cost method could be used. All recording and reports were to be of the amount at the time the transaction took place, whether one day or one hundred years ago.

In the recording function this rule still holds and is likely to do so for a long time to come. It ignores the falling value of money and assumes the currency unit of yesterday still has the same purchasing power as the unit of today.

When reporting, in the search for a greater realism, there are moves being made to adjust the results to bring all values to the current levels and to obtain a more correct view of progress and performance.

Convention of the true and fair view

A true and fair view is a convention pioneered by the United Kingdom for the publication of company accounts and the idea is spreading to other countries. Often regulations, when adhered to strictly, produce results which are legally correct but give a distorted view. To overcome this, rearrangement must be made so that the use of the legal format or a customary format does not hide undesirable features which ought to be shown up.

The Principles

With the rules specified it is now a matter of setting out the information for use. The recording is similar in all types of organizational structure and any differences arise from the need for different information to be extracted.

The objective must be clear reporting with enough detail for action to be taken.

Chapter Three

Organization of Business

As previously discussed the recording is always the same but the final results vary according to the type of organization. Three main groups exist in most countries. These are: the sole trader, where the owner takes all the risk and very often gives all the orders; the partnership, where two or more are gathered together with a view to making a profit; and lastly the forms of limited liability company, usually larger and involving a greater capital outlay but protecting the investors so that in the event of a catastrophe only the amount of the investment is lost irrespective of the amount of the debts.

The Sole Trader

Very often when a business starts it is one man either following his craft or employing several others to help him. From these small beginnings the business progresses until there is a need for administrative staff and expansion.

At this stage there is often a lack of capital and because of this many in this group fail to reach maturity and fall.

One trouble is the liability of the owner. No matter how large or small the debts it is the owner who will be responsible for their payment, whether or not he has to bring all his private possessions in as a part of the saving operation. To get the debts settled may mean being declared a bankrupt. In some countries this has lost some of the extreme penalty as after a certain number of years all restrictions are removed, the old debts are wiped out and the trader can begin again.

With this liability in existence it is very difficult for the sole trader to obtain capital beyond the amount of his own possessions and usually this becomes a restricting factor in the growth of the business.

Of course, when the business is very small the records likely to be kept are rudimentary and no matter how desirable the theoretical ideas are, the owner will want to concentrate on producing the goods rather than the paperwork. The luxury of a full set of books remains for the expansion period. Provided an accurate record is kept of all amounts paid out and received, the amounts owed and owing, and some record of the material and wages going into the product made or the service given, this should be sufficient.

At the end of the year, or more frequently, this can be summarized by the owner or by an accountant engaged by him to show how much profit has been made and the financial state of the business. This information will be used by the owner to see his progress and possibly by his bank, if there is any need for a loan.

It is likely the tax authorities will want a copy as well, for in most cases the tax liability is built up from the annual accounts.

There is still a further use. From the results the trader will be able to see if he is covering all of his costs and if he is making a suitable margin of profit. Then with the help of the information gathered on the cost of materials and the cost of labour (probably calculated from the time spent in making the product) he can calculate the future price base so his prices, while reflecting how much the customer is willing to pay, will not be below the total cost. Many small businesses have gone down through failing to use their results in this manner.

Two reports will be presented to him. One showing how his profit was arrived at and the other showing his financial status. The first may be called the TRADING AND PROFIT & LOSS ACCOUNT or the INCOME STATEMENT. Whichever it is, the revenue received by the business from sales will be shown and reduced by the expenses of the business classified under headings suitable for that business.

The financial status report may go under the name of the BALANCE SHEET or be called the FINANCIAL STATE-MENT. It will show the various possessions of the business, called assets, classified into groups for long and short term. These groupings will be dealt with in more detail later but it is enough to state here that information will be given on the amount of the stock, the cash held at the bank and the amounts owed to the business.

On the other hand the liabilities of the business will show – how much money is owed to the suppliers and others and, by far the most important fact, the amount of capital the owner has invested in the business.

This term capital is reserved purely for the investment put into a business and the idea is based on the concept of keeping the private affairs of the owner of the business divorced from the business affairs.

For the sole trader, it is as if, when he commenced in business, he took a part of his money and passed it over to the business for safe keeping. In the books and records, the business had to record this transaction as there is a liability by the business to repay the owner the sum invested at some time in the future, no matter how remote that may be.

If the owner expected to lose his money he could have given it to charity instead.

Also showing as a liability will be the profit earned by the business in the year and it may appear strange for this to be treated in this way. However, the reasoning is that by investing, the owner was hoping to increase the first investment by the profit and being the owner this excess belongs to him. Whether he draws it out or not, by showing it as a liability the business is merely acknowledging his ownership.

Two other aspects are brought in. While a profit is an addition to the capital, should the business have made a loss, then this is deducted from the capital being treated as a reduction of it.

The other aspect is the drawings – the withdrawal of capital or the drawing in anticipation of profit. It is considered that the reward of the owner of the business is not a salary or a wage but the receipt of profit and all that this item in the accounts shows is the extent of the amount taken out.

It would be perfectly admissible merely to show this in the accounts just as one figure of capital – the figure at the time the balance sheet was prepared. However, remembering that the object is to tell a story, a true story, it is helpful to show just how the increase or decrease in capital occurred and this ُ. done by first showing the capital at the beginning of the period, adding the profit and subtracting the withdrawals.

A similar idea is used for the profit and loss account. By showing an increased capital figure in the balance sheet it would be possible to calculate the profit for the year and to monitor it. All the profit and loss account does is to give a break-down of how the final profit or loss was arrived at for control and information purposes.

The Partnership

To provide the extra capital needed for running a business it may be necessary for two or more people to come together. They may both put in the necessary finance or one may put in the money and the other the expertise. The important feature is they intend to share any profit.

How they share the profit or, if they are unlucky, the losses, will be by the agreement made between them. Also in the agreement will be the rules for them to observe, to put in extra capital or to bring the partnership to an end.

In the United Kingdom, if they do make an agreement the provisions of the Partnership Act 1890 comes into force and they will have to share the profits equally no matter how many partners there are and how much they have contributed to the success of the firm.

Many of the partnerships are found in the area of personal services, such as doctors, lawyers and accountants, and in many cases they are not able to trade in any other form of organization, except as a sole trader.

As with the sole trader the liability of the partner is unlimited and should it be necessary to find money to pay the debts beyond the resources of the business the deficiency is first shared, but if one partner cannot pay, then his default is passed over to those remaining until their fortune is used up.

With this unlimited liability feature existing the possibility of the partnership being able to attract further capital, even if only loan capital, from beyond the resources of the partners, is as remote as if they had all been sole traders.

When preparing the accounts, the main difference from the accounts of the sole trader will be by the addition to the profit and loss account of a sub-section, known as an Appropriation Account, and in the capital section of the balance sheet. The amount of capital is kept fixed but the accumulations of profit less any drawings are shown for each partner as 'current' accounts.

This shows separately how much each partner contributed as capital, how much of the profit they have left in as a re-investment or how much they are drawing out.

The appropriation account is used as a device for showing how the profit was distributed to the various current accounts of the partners in accordance with the agreement, where this exists.

The limited partnership
To overcome the unlimited nature of the liability, a scheme was brought in at the end of the nineteenth century for one or more of the partners who only contributed the capital (and in return took some of the profit) to be able to limit his liability to the investment only. The overall number of partners was limited by law in the same way as the number is limited for all partnerships and at least one of the partners had to be a general partner, who took part in the management of the business but was responsible for the debts.

This arrangement brought in some risk capital from outside but did not help the creditability of the business when it came to acquiring loan facilities.

In the United Kingdom, although it was authorised by the Limited Partnership Act 1907, the idea did not gain much favour, probably due to the ease by which the private company with a limited liability for all the owners, whether they took part in the management or not, could be formed. On the continent of Europe this form is still found but as in Britain, its place has been taken a great extent by the private company.

Limited Liability Companies

When the Industrial Revolution came to Europe in the middle and latter half of the nineteenth century, the new enterprises found they were in need of large sums of money, often far more than one or two people were willing to risk out of their own resources. People were also worried as many still remembered the disasters of companies such as, in England, the South Sea Company, which gathered money together from many sources to trade and then developed grandiose ideas of taking the National Debt over from the Bank of England before they lost the lot and bankrupted many innocent people.

Money had to be found and the governments of the day created a form of corporation, controlled by the law, which would allow investment but would limit the liability of each investor to the amount put in and no more, whether the unpaid debts of the company were one pound or one million pounds.

Its deed of incorporation, in Britain called the Memorandum of Association, sets out the objectives and the power as well as giving the company a unique name. The formal rules by which it operates, not through its owners, but through professional managers (who might be owners as well) are found in, for Britain, the Articles of Association.

The various laws stipulate what is to go into the financial accounts for the company and fixes the period to be covered. In some countries the format of annual reports is also fixed.

As not all business ventures can be subject to the full rigours of the legal requirements without incurring excessive cost, different forms of company are allowed to be created at different levels and, more recently, concessions are being introduced on the amount of information to be disclosed. After all, in a small company where the owner of 99% of the share capital is also the only working director he should know a great deal of what is happening, whereas in the huge corporation with over half a million shareholders the needs are entirely different.

In the United Kingdom copies of the final accounts are available for all to see. Each company, whether private or public, must file a copy each year with the Registrar of Companies and for a small fee these can be inspected at one of his offices by any member of the public. The accounts filed are not as detailed as would be presented to the management but they do enable an opinion to be formed on the worth and performance of the company.

The private company
This style of company has been created to serve the needs of small business although many have grown far beyond the size originally intended to the extent that the latest European legislation now stipulates the disclosure requirements not by whether a company is private or public but by the level of turnover or the total value of the assets.

In most cases the number of shareholders is limited; in the United Kingdom this figure is 50. Because of the family nature of most of the small companies the directors often have the right given to them to refuse a transfer of shares to another person and, to make sure the shareholding can be controlled further, the private company is not allowed to offer its shares to the public.

There are other concessions to do with the minimum number of shareholders and directors permitted before the company can be operated.

Recently another form of private company has been gaining favour and this is the subsidiary of a public company, or sometimes of a private group of companies. The difficulty when assessing companies is finding out whether they are independent or controlled.

This information can be obtained by inspecting the files held by government departments and available to the public or by studying the information attached to the annual accounts to see if there is a substantial shareholding mentioned.

This is helped in the United Kingdom by the preparation of accounts for each individual company within a group and also for the group as a whole.

The public company
If a company cannot qualify as a private company it must be a public company and this is where the main benefits are to be found. The private company gave the benefits of the limited

21

liability to the small enterprise, allowing the craftsman to expand without the fear of losing all he had worked so hard to save.

The public company allows him to obtain the extra capital needed to make his product in quantities which will not only give a satisfactory return on the money put in by the shareholders but will give the managers of the company enough incentive as well.

A public company is able to reach out to invite the public to subscribe for the shares, to take part in risky enterprises which they would not have the power or resources to do by other means.

The public company, nowadays, also acts as a channel for the savings of the public in general to be diverted to help finance industry though the investment of the premiums received by insurance companies and the contributions received by pension funds.

The quoted public company

Just because a company is a public company does not mean a person can obtain shares in it. All that is meant is, if the company wants funds, it can go to the public to get them.

This could be both difficult and costly. Firstly the buyer must be found and secondly having found him he must be induced to buy. One of the benefits he will want is the ability to sell his share should he not be satisfied with the performance or should he need to use his money for another purpose in an emergency.

The place to do this is the Stock Exchange. Its history is another matter but over the years most exchanges have built up reputations for fair dealing and they have no intention of losing them. They will allow only reputable shares to be dealt with through a particular exchange, and to get a listing the company has to supply enough financial information to the exchange to prove its worth. Once accepted it needs to comply with the rules to stay listed.

It is probably the influence of the stock exchange listing which makes the public company disclose more information in the annual accounts than is required by law and is shaping the form of those accounts today.

Company accounts

Other than the general disclosure, the basic pattern of the company accounts is as for the sole trader and the partnership, although what is developed for the quoted public company today will find its way into the other accounts tomorrow.

Once again the main difference is in the capital sector. With so many owners it would be impossible to show the situation of each one and so, as they all get identical dividends for each share they own, totals are given.

The share capital is shown separately in total. In Britain this is shown at the nominal or par value. Each share must be given a value at the time of issue and dividends are calculated on this basis.

In the same way as the sole trader was entitled to the profits, the shareholders are entitled to the profits which are left in the business and not paid out as dividend. In fact it is only one of the classes of shareholder that gets this residual treatment but the explanation of the differences can wait until a later stage.

These undistributed profits together with some other amounts which also belong eventually to the shareholders are kept under certain classifications and, with the shares, form the 'shareholders' worth' in the company. If the total worth is divided by the number of shares issued, a book value of the shares can be found.

Many countries do not follow this separate classification but follow the structure used by the sole trader and add the undistributed profit to the share value to give one capital sum. These shares are known as shares of 'no par value' and this is the system used in the United States of America.

Chapter Four

Method of Recording

Dual entry was one of the concepts and through it can be understood the principle of double entry bookkeeping, how the various accounts are related to each other, how a balance sheet is built up and the structure of the accounting records.

It is the simple balance sheet which is the starting point, and although the system is basically for manually kept accounts, it is adapted through to the computer-based systems. The forms may change but the system remains.

A Simple Case

William Bloggins had for years worked as an assistant in a butcher's shop, carefully saving his money and dreaming of the day when he could open his own shop and advertise around the town 'Bloggins for Meat'. Gradually his savings reached £5,000 and this he felt was sufficient for lift-off. He had done all his planning, cash flows, budgeting and other financial matters. He had obtained all the necessary licences, planning consents and had found just the right shop to rent.

He saw his bank manager and arranged for a transfer of the £5,000 to a new account to be opened and called W. Bloggins, Butchery Account. He had in fact put in capital for the business and if a balance sheet were constructed after the transaction it would show as in fig. 1, an asset owned by the business of £5,000 in cash at bank and a recorded liability of £5,000 as capital from Bill Bloggins in his personal capacity.

| Cash at Bank | £5000 | Capital – W. Bloggins | £5000 |

Fig. 1   Initial balance sheet.

24

Note how there is equilibrium with one side balancing the other; a feature which must be maintained throughout. In fact at this stage it can be shown:

ASSETS (Cash at bank) = LIABILITIES (Capital)

The next stage was to arrange the renting of the shop and for this he paid from his bank three months rent in advance – £250. He reduced his asset of cash by £250 and recorded an expense of £250 under the classification of RENT (fig. 2).

Cash at Bank	£4,750	Capital – W. Bloggins	£5,000
Rent paid	250		
	£5,000		£5,000

Fig. 2   Balance sheet after rent paid.

It may seem peculiar that a payment out can be classed as an asset but what Butcher Bloggins purchased was the right to use the premises for three months.

What has occurred above is a rearrangement of the assets with no effect on the liabilities. Each side of the balance sheet adds up to equal the other, so equilibrium is maintained and the equation still holds.

At the next stage the shop is fitted, the refrigerators hired and the initial stock of meat is purchased. Once again, when shown in balance sheet form, it is a rearrangement of the asset side with the cash at the bank being reduced (fig. 3).

Cash at Bank	£1,700	Capital – W. Bloggins	£5,000
Rent paid	250		
Shopfittings	1,000		
Hire of refrigerators	50		
Purchase of meat	2,000		
	£5,000		£5,000

Fig. 3   Balance after shopfitting.

Method of Recording

The two sides amount to the same total so the equation is still holding.

Finally opening day arrives and meat to the value of £500 is sold and this amount is paid into the bank immediately the shop closes for the night. On the same day some more meat was ordered and delivered ready for the next day but instead of paying cash it was purchased on credit, use now and pay later.

This means the business has incurred a further liability. Where an amount is owed by a business the person to whom it is owed is termed a CREDITOR.

The situation is now that the meat purchased has increased by £1,500 and the liabilities are increased by a creditor for £1,500.

The other transaction must also be recorded with an increase in the cash of £500 for the meat sold and on the other side sales of £500 shown. It may seem strange to have sales treated as a liability but for an explanation it is necessary to examine the nature of profit and its relationship to the sales.

As agreed before, the profit eventually belongs to the owner of the business and the business must record this liability. Hence profit will show as a liability.

Profit is made up of the revenue from sales earned by the business less the cost of those sales – the expenses incurred by the business. If there is a profit, the sales value will exceed the expenses and from this it is easy to reason that the sales should be treated as a liability being merely a part of profit.

The balance sheet will now appear as in fig. 4.

Cash at Bank	£2,200	Capital – W. Bloggins	£5,000
Rent paid	250	Sale of Meat	500
Shopfittings	1,000	Creditor	1,500
Hire of refrigerator	50		
Purchase of Meat (2,000+1,500)	3,500		
	£7,000		£7,000

Fig. 4   Balance after a day's trading.

26

As both sides are still equal, the equation is satisfied but it is now entirely clear that within the liabilities there is more than one type.

Custom requires the long term liabilities to be kept separate from the rest and the liability to the owner is the longest of them all so it is separated and put under the heading CAPITAL leaving the rest still called LIABILITIES.

The equation now becomes:

$$ASSETS = CAPITAL + LIABILITIES$$

On the second day of business the transactions were a further sale of meat for cash of £750 – increase asset of cash £750 and increase sales by £750 – and a further sale of meat valued at £320 to a local hotel.

The hotel does not pay immediately and has asked for trade credit, a request which is granted. The hotel is now a DEBTOR for £320 to the business. As an acknowledged debt is the right to obtain the cash at a later date, it is treated as an asset. It is as if the customer is keeping the amount on behalf of the trader for a short period instead of its being left in his bank.

As no money was passed over the cash at bank is unaltered but there is now an additional asset of a debtor for £320, and as this is as good a sale as any other, the sales total rises by the £320.

To construct a balance sheet after each transaction would not have been practical so an alternative was devised. Each class of transaction was given a separate sheet where all like items could be gathered so at the end of the period it would be easy to summarise all the receipts or expenditure under that heading. Each classification is called an account.

So that the sheet would not be just a jumble of figures just two columns were used, one for each side of the sheet, which had been divided down the centre.

The left hand side was called the DEBIT side and the right hand, the CREDIT. To debit an item meant to make an entry on the debit side of the account and nothing more, to credit was to enter on the right hand side. The words can be used either as nouns or verbs.

A traditional layout is shown in fig. 5.

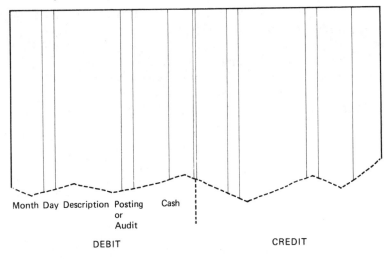

Fig. 5 *Traditional layout of ledger sheet.*

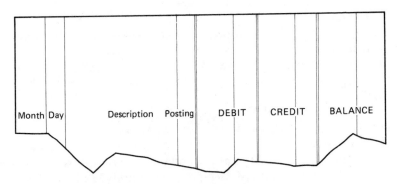

Fig. 6 *Alternative layout of ledger sheet.*

Sometimes an alternative layout is found in some manual systems which are based on a time-saving scheme with two or more accounts being completed at the same time. In this type there are three columns on an account. The layout is shown in fig. 6. The account is not divided as before and the first column coming from the left is for the debits, the second which is the middle column is for the credits and the third, on the extreme right for the balance.

One advantage is that the balance is found after each entry and it is easy to check the arithmetic on each sheet merely by adding the debits, then the credits and making sure the difference agrees with the last column.

This is all there is to the basic idea of double entry bookkeeping and it is a matter of accurate work to keep the books in balance. Often for the learner there needs to be a decision as to

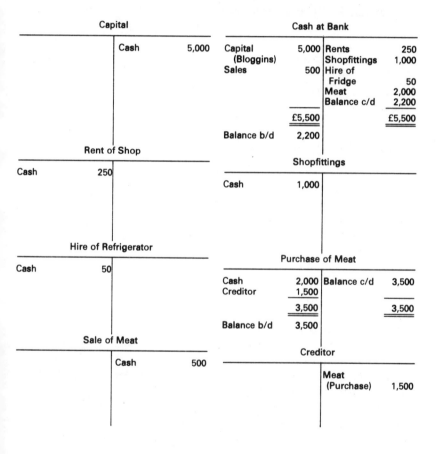

Fig. 7 Effects of debits and credits on a cash account.

whether an item should be a debit or a credit and there are many aids devised.

One is to remember that in the cash account all receipts are entered on the debit side and all payments are credits. If the transaction can be thought out as if it concerned cash, although neither aspect does, it may solve some problems.

A chart showing the effect of debits and credits is shown in fig. 7.

In fig. 7 the transactions for Bloggins the Butcher have converted from being all in one account into several accounts and taken one step further to be totalled where necessary and the balances calculated and, as the term is, 'brought down'.

The skeleton account form is known as 'T' accounts and is often used in teaching where it is not practical to put all the detail on.

Collecting the Ledger Together

Each classification has its own account and the number of accounts opened is a choice made by management when they decide on the groupings. Collectively all the accounts are termed THE LEDGER. Originally this was a bound book but now it may be a collection of machine accounting cards, a series of punched cards or a magnetic strip of plastic from a computer or just a magnetized stripe.

When the ledger was bound in one cover it presented difficulties as the business expanded and more than one person wanted to work on it at the same time, and to accommodate all the accounts it had to be bulky.

A solution was found which was to take away the account with the most transactions, the cash account, and to put it into a separate binding to become the cash book. What has to be remembered is that this is an account, really a part of the ledger, and the balance must be included when finalizing the accounts.

The next to go were the personal accounts, the accounts with names of customers or suppliers, and these became two separate subsidiary ledgers – the SALES LEDGER for the customers and the BOUGHT LEDGER for the suppliers. Sometimes if the accounts are numerous they are subdivided even further into alphabetical or geographical splits, according to the needs of efficient management.

A typical breakdown of the ledger is shown in fig. 8.

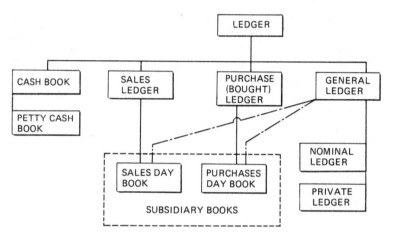

Fig. 8   A possible division of the ledger and the relationship of the subsidiary books.

The subsidiary books

It was in the ledger that all the financial secrets of the business were held so it needed special control and care. Not every clerk could have access and so the detail of each entry was first entered into DAY BOOKS, which were, as the name implies, books for entering day by day transactions. The amounts were posted periodically to the ledgers.

Gradually it was realized this created a great deal of extra work and certain accounts, for example the sales account, contained a lot of unnecessary detail.

Using the example of the sales account, the problem was solved by first listing all the sales invoices in a special day-book confined to sales only. From this list, each entry had to be posted to the appropriate customer account in the Sales

Ledger, for it was essential to know exactly how much each customer owed (later, on payment, the cash was posted to customer's account as well, to reduce the debt). It was not essential to know in the Sales Account either the amount of each invoice or the name of the customer, so if the total of the Sales Day-book was taken periodically and posted to the Sales Account, this would be sufficient. Detail was eliminated and double-entry was satisfied as the total of the debits made on the various accounts was equal to the one credit in the Sales Account.

A similar procedure was used for the purchases and these systems are still used today in the manual systems for the smaller business.

Trying to balance

The bookkeeper likes to know if the amounts have been entered properly and that all the debits are where debits should be. To check this he extracts a TRIAL BALANCE.

He makes a list of all the accounts in the ledger and on the right hand side of the sheet makes two cash columns; left hand for the debit balances and the right for the credit balances.

Then each account is totalled and the balance noted in the trial balance as the amount and whether it is debit or credit.

A debit balance results when the total of the entries on the debit side exceeds the total on the credit side and a credit balance results when the credit total is excessive.

If the totals of both columns agree then all the debits and credits have been entered correctly. It also shows that the balances have been extracted correctly and the additions are correct.

It does not show if the amounts have been entered into the correct account; if the original information was incorrect; if an item has been omitted entirely and there has been a compensating error.

Assuming it balances and appears to be in order, the bookkeeper can relax. His task is done for that period and the accountant takes over.

When all the transactions are scattered over many accounts in the ledger they do not tell a coherent story about the state of the finances. They need to be collated and arranged for presentation and the trial balance assists in this stage.

As it must contain the balance extracted from each account in the ledger the collating part of the final procedure is done and the accountant can rearrange these balances to his need and make the necessary adjustments to make sure only expense or revenue for the period being reviewed is included.

Control accounts

One major refinement was necessary. If all the accounts had to be listed separately in the trial balance the list would not only be exceedingly long but if there were any errors it would be an onerous task to find them.

By taking the divisions of the ledger and providing a check on their accuracy, either internally or externally to the business, is the solution.

For the petty cash simply add up the cash. The same procedure is needed for any cash kept out of the bank and controlled through the cash book.

For the bank section of the cash book, a reconciliation with the detailed statement from the bank is sufficient. It has to be a reconciliation as due to the clearing system for cheques it takes several days from when the cheque is issued until it is paid by the branch where the bank account is kept.

This leaves the personal ledgers, and sometimes other subsidiary ledgers where the accounting system is large. They are made self-balancing, a check is made internally to make sure the postings are correct and only the total of the balances in the sub-ledger is put into the main trial balance.

To understand the procedure, it is necessary to realize that the whole of the checking is carried out by using totals.

First a 'trial' balance is made of all the accounts within the particular ledger but instead of the totals of the debit balances being equal to the credit balances, one is subtracted from the other to show the difference.

Then a totals account is constructed for all the items posted to the ledger. Again taking the sales ledger as an example, the total of the sales day-book is put to the debit (all totals are put on the same side as they appear in the individual accounts).

Method of Recording

The total of all cash received from customers in payment during the period is put to the credit. The totals of adjustments such as credit notes issued and set-offs against purchases are put to the appropriate side and an opening balance brought in (the agreed totals at the end of the previous period). Then a balance is taken and if all is correct this should equal the total of the individual accounts.

Chapter Five

Financial Summaries

At least once in every twelve months a business must produce final accounts. This magic figure is not just conjured out of the air but is the normal requirement of company legislation, the tax authorities and, when money has been borrowed, the bank manager.

Many businesses produce their summaries at much shorter intervals but normally these do not have the same degree of accuracy and are better adapted for control purposes, although a recent trend is for the quoted public companies to publish some accounts either at six months or quarterly.

There is no reason why the accounts should be produced to coincide with a calendar month or the beginning of a calendar year provided they are produced at a consistent date. In the United Kingdom a company can choose which ever date it likes and must inform the government registry of this, but if it fails to give the necessary notice, the financial year will have to end on 31 March in each year.

Final Accounts

A set of final accounts is considered to mean two main statements. The balance sheet to show the financial state at a given date, and the profit and loss account to give the breakdown of the profit figure. Various names are given to these statements in different parts of the world but all seem to be agreed these are the minimum needed to monitor the progress of a business.

They suffer from one limitation. They are historical and if their preparation is slow they become ancient history so that by the time they are published the character of the business has changed to such an extent that the results bear no relationship to reality.

Even with this limitation they are often the only means available for those outside the business to know what is happening within.

Profit and loss account

Sometimes known as the Income Statement this summary is really a readable version of the summary account kept within the ledger. At the end of a year, in the set of books kept by the purist, the balances on all the expense and revenue accounts are transferred to the profit and loss account.

It is, for publication purposes, several sub-accounts joined together and, to maintain commercial confidentiality, certain parts are retained for use by the management and the rest can be free for all.

The first subdivision is the MANUFACTURING ACCOUNT used if this activity is a part of the business. It gives in global terms the amount of materials used in production, the labour charges and the overhead charges incurred in running the production unit. Where there is integrated accounting this has a direct link and can be reconciled with the costing system.

The final figure will be the cost of the finished goods and this is transferred to the next subdivision, the TRADING ACCOUNT. Its purpose is to highlight the profit margin made on trading, on the buying and selling of goods.

Gross profit is the aim and this is found by subtracting from the sales or revenue the cost of those sales. This is usually made up from the opening stock plus the purchases in the year less the stock of saleable goods at the end.

There have to be variations for the business which provides a service rather than sells a product.

From the trading account the gross profit is caried down into the main profit and loss account where it is reduced by the expenses incurred in running the business. These are mainly the selling and distribution costs, the administrative costs and the financial costs. Also into this section is taken any sundry income which is earned by the secondary activities of the business. This could include the rent received from the letting of surplus accommodation or the income from investments.

The resultant figure is the Net Profit which often under the guise of the term 'Operating Profit' is the starting off point for the published Profit and Loss Accounts in Company Financial Reporting. Above the net profit is information which has no practical use to the external user with the exception of the competitors.

If the business is belonging to a sole trader it is the net profit which is taken directly to the capital account to increase the owner's worth in the business.

For partnerships and corporations with their many owners a final subdivision, the APPROPRIATION ACCOUNT, is produced.

This shows how the profit is distributed. It shows how much has been taken for taxes, how much is put into reserve for future use or re-investment in the business and how much, for a company, is paid out as dividend. In the partnership accounts instead of dividend the appropriation account will detail the amounts to be transferred to each partner's current account for the share of profits, any interest paid on the capital put into the business and any salary paid to a partner to compensate for an extra work effort.

Authorized Capital			*Fixed Assets*		
15,000 Ordinary shares			Plant and Machinery		
of £1 each		£15,000	at cost		37,079
			Less depreciation		3,578
Issued Capital					33,501
10,000 Ordinary shares					
of £1 each, fully paid		10,000			
General Reserve		5,000			
Profit and Loss Account		26,680	*Current Assets*		
		41,680	Stocks and Work in		
			progress	15,892	
10% Debentures		10,000	Trade Debtors	10,865	
Current Liabilities			Cash	534	
Trade Creditors	2,573				
Corporation Tax	4,539				27,291
Proposed dividend	2,000	9,112			
		£60,792			£60,792

Fig. 9   Balance sheet for XYZ Ltd. as at 31 December 19———

The balance sheet

Once the net profit, or for companies once the profit to be retained, has been calculated the Balance Sheet (or Financial Statement as it is called in some parts) can be prepared. This shows all the assets and liabilities of the business classified to suit the business and to show the long and short term situation.

An example of a simple balance sheet is shown in fig.9 and

Opening Stock of raw materials	2,543		Cost of Production transferred to	
Purchases	13,294	16,837	Trading Account	34,934
Less Closing Stock		2,995		
Direct Materials		13,842		
Direct Wages		15,497		
Prime Cost		29,339		
Sundry Factory Overheads		5,322		
		34,661		
Adjust for Work in Progress				
Opening	3,297			
Closing	3,024	273		
Cost of Production		£34,934		£34,934
Opening Stock of finished goods		10,310	Sales	54,329
Production for year		34,934		
		45,244		
Less Closing Stock		9,873		
Cost of Goods sold		35,371		
Gross Profit carried to Profit & Loss Account		18,958		
		£54,329		£54,329
Selling Expense		3,542	Gross Profits brought down	18,958
Administration Expenses		6,784		
Net Profits carried down		8,632		
		£18,958		£18,958
Corporation Tax		4,539	Net Profits b/d.	8,632
Proposed Dividend		2,000	Profit & Loss Account	24,587
Retained Profit		26,680		
		£33,219		£33,219

Fig. 10   Manufacturing, trading and profit and loss account of XYZ Ltd. for the year ending 31 December 19——.

the manufacturing, trading, profit and loss, and appropriation accounts which made up the profit are in fig. 10.

The contents of the balance sheet will be discussed in detail when the disclosure requirements are examined later in the sections on financial accounting.

Accruals and Prepayment

To comply with the concept of relating the expenses and revenue together so that the true cost of operating can be produced, the balances in the various accounts need to be adjusted.

This is the task of the accountant and is carried out once the trial balance has been agreed.

ACCRUALS occur when an expense has been incurred but for various reasons it was not possible to set up the entry in the books by the end of the year. For example, the charge is for a service which is continuous, such as the supply of electricity, and the bill when it comes in during the following year covers current used in both periods.

The charge has to be proportioned either by the amount of the current used or if this cannot be found, in some other fair manner, probably on a time basis. The amount for the consumption in the period is added to the existing electricity expense and a liability is created acknowledging there is amount due to the supplier. This created liability will form a part of the Sundry Creditors item or the Accruals item in the Balance Sheet.

Other examples of accruals will be where wages are due. This may occur if the end of the financial year does not coincide with the end of the working week or the employees work with a week's wages in hand. Some forms of taxes due will come under this category.

On the other hand where there has been a prepayment, such as for insurance, the expense already booked to the account in the ledger must be reduced to get the amount 'consumed' in the year.

A proportion is taken off and carried forward to be an expense in the following period. This is termed as a

PREPAYMENT and is shown in the balance sheet as such, or under the heading of 'Sundry Debtors'.

The idea of showing this as an asset and a debtor is that, should the business not be able to proceed with the rest of the contract concerned, it can claim a refund. This is being acknowledged in the statement.

Provisions

When a company or other business is producing its final accounts, it is only right for all the possible liabilities to be included in case the reader or user of the accounts obtains an over-optimistic opinion of the situation.

Where the bills which arrive too late are concerned, these are dealt with in the Accruals, but there are other items, very often of greater amount, which although an invoice will not be sent from a supplier, represent a future charge to the business. Sometimes this liability cannot be calculated to the last penny but it is still present and provision for this must be made against the profit so that, by accident, the amount is not paid out to the owners as profit and cause possible difficulties when it becomes a reality.

PROVISIONS are made and shown in the balance sheet with the other liabilities for such items as future contributions to a pension fund or for the repair of a building.

One form of provision which is not shown separately is the 'Provision for doubtful Debts'. In most businesses there are some customers whose ability to pay is most doubtful and it would be wrong to treat the sales concerned, and the profit coming from those sales, as certain and available for distribution until the payment is made. The amounts concerned are found by either examining the list of debtors or as often in the large concern with numerous customers a percentage based on statistical calculations of past defaults is provided.

For accounting purposes the profit is reduced by the amount of the provision and this is then deducted from the total of the debtors so that the amount in the balance sheet shows only the value of the debts the business expects to collect.

Should any of the debts be bad, that is they can never be

collected, they are treated as a charge against the profit in the period when it was agreed they would not be paid.

Another provision which is dealt with in a separate manner is for depreciation of assets but this will be explained after 'reserves'.

Reserves

As with an individual, a business does not always have to spend all it earns. It has the opportunity to save and the amount put aside for this purpose is termed a RESERVE.

It may be an amount set aside for a specific purpose occurring in the future where neither the timing nor the final amount is certain. For example a 'Reserve for Plant Replacement'. Or, it may be merely savings which are re-invested into the business instead of being distributed in case, at some time, they need to be called upon. This is usually termed the 'General Reserve'.

A further form found in corporate accounting is the 'Retained Profit' or as it is sometimes headed in the balance sheet, 'Profit and Loss Account'.

This is the small amount left over in the appropriation account after the distributions have been made, the tax provided and the amounts made to specific reserves. It belongs to the shareholders so must appear with the reserves as a liability. Custom decrees that transfers to specific reserves are normally rounded off to the thousand or even ten thousand pounds according to the size of the business.

For company purposes the reserves are classified under two main headings, CAPITAL RESERVES and REVENUE RESERVES. The former usually arise from either capital transaction such as a premium paid on the issue of shares or from revaluations of assets. In both cases it is considered bad practice and often against the law to make these amounts available for dividend.

In the first example, as the premium was taken from the shareholders when they paid for their shares, it would be futile to be able to pay the amount back to them as profit.

In the second case the revaluing of an asset is not realizing a profit but merely a book adjustment to make the balance sheet reflect realistic values. As the asset has not been sold no money is available from it for use.

While the capital reserves are not available for dividends the revenue reserves being created from profits are free to return to the profits and, if desired, be paid out of the company through dividends.

One very important fact to remember about reserves (and to a certain extent about provisions) is that they do not represent free money in the business even if they did originate as surplus profits. They are amounts which have been *re-invested* in the business and the money which originally came from the earnings to give the surplus has been used over time to purchase new assets or has been used to pay wages and to buy more stock to finance further production.

Depreciation

Before the annual accounts can be completed provision must be made for DEPRECIATION of the fixed assets. This has nothing to do with the loss in value through use, as defined by the economists, but the recovery of the initial expenditure on the asset by instalments spread over the estimated life of the item.

The theory is, a part of the initial expenditure is consumed each year in generating profits and it is only fair that the profits for the year should treat this amount as an expense. This stops the amount being made available for distribution and maintains the capital at the original level.

Of course, the provision must be based on the estimated life as it could only be certain if no charge was made until the asset was scrapped and all the accounts adjusted over the previous years to reflect a proportion of the cost. This is impractical. On the other hand, unless a charge is made the profits for the year have not taken in all the expense of the business and then the results would not be showing a true and fair view.

There are many methods of calculating depreciation. All have their devotees and are suitable for certain circumstances.

The most popular method and probably the most easy to operate is the straight line method. Each year a fixed amount is charged and this is calculated by taking the estimated life in years and dividing this number into the cost less an estimation of the scrap value at the end of its life. The resultant figure is then expressed as a percentage of the cost.

In modern practice the scrap value is usually ignored as with inflation and the rapid advance of technology no reliable estimate can be made.

Should there be too much depreciation, due to a good disposal price or an under-depreciation when the asset has to be replaced or disposed of before the end of its estimated life, then, the profit or loss created is treated as an extraordinary item (one that is not part of the trading) in the profit and loss account in the year of the disposal.

It is usual to classify the assets into groups and to apply an agreed percentage rate to the whole of that group and not to take each asset separately.

An example of the application of the straight line method is in fig. 11.

Cost of Asset	£10,000
Expected life	5 years
Year 0 (cost)	£10,000
Year 1 depreciation @ 20%	2,000
Written down value	8,000
Year 2 depreciation	2,000
Written down value	6,000
Year 3 depreciation	2,000
Written down value	4,000
Year 4 depreciation	2,000
Written down value	2,000
Year 5 depreciation	2,000

Fig. 11   Example of straight line depreciation.

As an alternative the reducing balance method is used. In this an agreed percentage is applied to the written down value of the asset each year.

The written down value is book value of the asset remaining after deducting the accumulated depreciation. This amount is the total of the depreciation charged to the assets concerned from the time of purchase.

An accurate calculation of the rate to be applied is by the formula:

$$1 - \sqrt[n]{\frac{s}{c}}$$

where *n* is the number of years; *s* is the scrap value and *c* is the original cost.

In practice the percentage is found by trial and error and is about twice the percentage needed to write off the cost over the same number of years using the straight line methods.

While this method does have the advantage of probably reflecting the true charge to the profits for the year, its practical use has been diminished since 1969 in the United Kingdom by the requirement for companies to show in their published accounts the original cost and the accumulated depreciation for each class of asset.

The advantage of the reducing balance nethod is in taking the overall charge to the business. In the early years when the repair costs are low the depreciation is high. The position is gradually reversed as the estimated life comes to an end. As the repairs are considered to be used in maintaining the asset up to

Cost of Asset	£10,000
Rate of depreciation	40% per annum
Year 0 (cost)	£10,000
Year 1 depreciation	4,000
Written down value	6,000
Year 2 depreciation	2,400
Written down value	3,600
Year 3 depreciation	1,440
Written down value	2,160
Year 4 depreciation	864
Written down value	1,296
Year 5 depreciation	518
Written down value	778 and so on

Fig. 12   Example of the reducing balance method of depreciation.

the required standard it is also maintaining the capital invest-ment level, as is depreciation and so the total charge of these two is more realistic.

An example of the effect of the reducing balance method over a five year period is shown in fig.12.

Other methods of calculating depreciation are the revalua-tion method and methods based on use such as the machine hour, etc. Revaluation is often used for small tools or in the catering industry for crockery and glassware. The asset is valued at the end of the year and amount taken from the value at the beginning of the year. Any fall in value is treated as depreciation.

Fixed and Current Assets

In the discussion of depreciation, fixed assets were mentioned but the term was not explained.

In every business there are assets which are used to generate profits and there are those which are actually used up in the generation of the profit.

The first are the FIXED ASSETS and it is the intention of the business that they will last for more than one financial year. They are usually of a permanent nature such as buildings, plant and machinery, motor vehicles and furniture and fittings. All of these contribute to the earning of the profit but do not become consumed directly.

On the other hand there are assets which are likely to change their value through use during the next period and in fact if they do not, the business is likely to be in serious trouble or to have stopped trading altogether. In the main these assets are absorbed in the trading or derive from trading and include the stock-in-trade, debtors, cash and near cash, such as temporary investments and deposits. These are the CURRENT ASSETS.

A similar situation applies to the liabilities but these are divided into the LONG-TERM LIABILITIES and the CUR-RENT LIABILITIES.

The long-term liabilities are those which are not due in the next financial period and include items such as the loan capital, the share capital and the reserves (although really they should still be kept under the capital heading), deferred taxation, and any other negotiated long term borrowings.

The current liabilities are those expected to be paid off in the next year including the trade creditors, the current taxation and the dividend to the shareholders.

Capital and Revenue Expenditure

Other terms which need to be mentioned are capital and revenue expenditure.

CAPITAL EXPENDITURE is, as implied, the spending on capital items such as the fixed assets, and its source is usually the long-term capital from either the share issues or the borrowings.

REVENUE EXPENDITURE is the expenditure incurred to generate the revenue and will include the purchase of materials, labour and all the other expense needed to operate the business from day to day. It forms a part of what is termed the working capital and although it is more satisfactory if the bulk is financed from the long-term and more fixed capital sources, the fluctuations can be financed from the temporary sources such as bank overdrafts and suppliers' credit.

The term working capital refers to the capital or finance used in operating the business, to finance the current assets and the current liabilities, as opposed to the fixed capital which is used for the financing of the assets of a more durable nature.

The Format of Balance Sheets

Up until now no reference has been made to the format of the balance sheet. In the beginning of chapter four the balance sheets were shown with the assets on the same side – the left – as in the books or records of account. When it came to an example, in fig. 9, the assets appeared on the right and the capital and liabilities on the left.

While it does not really matter which side is used from the point of view of balancing the assets against the liabilities, it does cause confusion especially as the placing of the assets on the right, the opposite to the books, was the method adopted in

England for many years. In most other parts of the world the assets were placed on the left although the English justification seems to be that by using the opposite format from the books it shows the balance sheet to be a statement and not a consolidated copy of the books.

With the development of international trade it came to be recognized that the horizontal format was confusing whichever way around it was prepared. The lay-reader would find it very difficult to relate the items on one side to those on the other.

As an alternative the vertical format has been developed.

The balance sheet is divided into two sections, one following the other, and the order in which they appear is left to the management preparing the accounts, for they can be read just as well either way.

Balance Sheet of XYZ Ltd as at 31 December 19—			
Fixed Assets			
Plant & Machinery at cost		£37,079	
Less Depreciation to date		3,578	33,501
Current Assets			
Stocks and Work in Progress		15,892	
Trade Debtors		10,865	
Cash		534	
		27,291	
Less Current Liabilities			
Trade Creditors	2,573		
Corporation Tax	4,539		
Proposed Dividends	2,000	9,112	18,179
NET CAPITAL EMPLOYED			£51,680
FINANCED BY			
Authorized Capital			
15,000 Ordinary Shares of £1 each			£15,000
Issued Capital			
10,000 Ordinary Shares of £1 each, fully paid			£10,000
General Reserve			5,000
Profit and Loss Account			26,680
			41,680
10% Debenture			10,000
			£51,680

Fig. 13   Vertical format of balance sheet previously shown in a horizontal format in fig. 9.

The two sections show, firstly, the sources of the finance and, secondly, how the capital has been employed. Fig. 13 converts the previous horizontal format into the vertical.

The financing sector includes the share capital, the reserves, the long-term borrowings and any deferred liabilities. The capital employed has the fixed assets, any investments and the current assets less the current liabilities. This last part is very useful when interpreting the accounts as the current assets less the current liabilities is the amount of the working capital, the amount the business uses to finance its operations.

It is also becoming the practice to use the vertical format in the profit and loss account and it is becoming rare to find the horizontal format used in the published accounts of the quoted companies. The lay-out starts with the sales and reduces the figure in turn by the costs of sales from the trading account and then by the costs of operation to give the net profit.

Then by deducting the tax for the year the impact of tax is shown, and after showing the dividend to be paid, the remaining figure is the retained profit for the reserves, rather than merely the total of a column of figures. This is shown in fig. 14.

Sales		£54,329
Less *Cost of Goods sold*:		
Opening Stock of finished goods	10,310	
Factory production for year	34,934	
	45,244	
Less Closing Stock	9,873	35,371
GROSS PROFIT		18,958
Less:		
Selling Expense	3,542	
Administration Expense	6,784	10,326
NET PROFIT		8,632
Corporation Tax		4,539
PROFIT AFTER TAX		4,093
Proposed Dividend		2,000
		2,093
Previous balance on profit and loss account		24,587
Retained Profit		£26,680

Fig. 14   Trading and profit and loss account of XYZ Ltd. for the year ending 31 December 19——. This is the vertical format version of the account shown in horizontal format in fig. 10.

Chapter Six

Basic Costing

In the previous chapters the recording, the collating and the reporting of the financial transactions have been brought together to show how a business is progressing.

This information is used in the making of investment decisions by readers of the final accounts who cannot have access to the internal workings of the business, to monitor progress and for inter-business comparisons.

Useful as this is for obtaining an overall view of what is happening and for exercising a restricted degree of control, more information is needed if there is to be firm control of the day-to-day operations. Decisions have to be made which require detailed information to be supplied. It is no use to divide the amounts produced by the financial accounts by the number of articles produced and expect to get meaningful figures. The average will be produced but this will not show up any waste or inefficiency in a particular sector.

The solution has been the development of management accounting – the supply of information to management, based on the operating facts, for them to decide on the corrections needed to keep the organization within its targets.

As with the financial transactions the first stage is recording and this is termed COSTING. It follows the same rules as the financial accounting and is collated and reported upon as before.

What is Costing?

A definition of costing has been given as the finding of the cost of a unit of production but in fact the process can go further, controlling not only the direct aspect but also the extra services needed to make a business operate.

To achieve the aim of knowing the cost of each unit in total it is possible to find the cost of each process, or even each sub-process, in manufacture and then to break this down further and find out how much material has been used or how many hours (or minutes) of labour were involved.

Once again, the concept of materiality must be considered. There must be a decision made on how far the detail is needed. It costs money to record, it takes time to record, and unless the information is to be used effectively, it is a waste to extract it in the first place.

In the recent past, with the employment of clerical labour, it was fairly easy to measure the cost of costing but today with the coming of computers many of the costs are concealed.

What has to be remembered is that even the time taken by the operative to mark up a job sheet is costing money and if it is realized that the detail will not be used then, very soon, the times and other information shown will cease to be accurate and the whole system will be distorted to become a complete waste of money.

Gathering the Costs

The modern tendency is to gather costs at convenient points along the production system at what are known as cost centres. They may be at a workbench, a particular machine, a group of machines or even a complete department.

Under some costing systems information is required not only about the production of goods but also about the production of services.

There is no reason why services should not be costed. They represent expenditure by the business and this needs to be planned and controlled just as vigorously as the cost of producing goods.

Sometimes the costs are gathered to a higher point called a profit centre. This happens when it is useful to be able to monitor the build up of the profit element in the production cycle.

This usually forms a part of what is termed RESPONSI-BILITY ACCOUNTING.

Once, only the boss at the top made the decisions and nobody else was considered to have the capacity to do this. Such an attitude is possible when there are only two or three employees but even with an organization as small as this he cannot be present all the time. He may be out visiting a customer, be sick or it may be that the business is too big for him to be in all places at once.

He has to delegate and make an employee responsible for the carrying out of a particular task, so that when he is not there the whole place does not grind to a halt. While it is good practice for a task to be delegated, the person now responsible for carrying it out needs to know, just as much as does the boss, what is happening.

This dividing up of the information to be supplied at the different levels, according to the decisions at each level, is known as responsibility accounting.

Direct costs

The first convenient method used in the gathering of costs at the various centres is to obtain the direct costs, also known as the prime costs.

There are two aspects of any cost. One part can be traced to the product or service and identified within it but the other, although essential, cannot be traced and most usually needs to be allocated on a proportional basis. The first is the direct cost and the second the indirect.

Within both groups there are said to be three component parts; the material element, the labour element and the expenses element. All three do not have to be present at the same time – this depends upon the unit being costed. They are usually referred to as direct materials, direct labour and direct expenses.

Direct materials and direct labour are self-explanatory but the direct expenses do lead to some confusion with the indirect expenses. This comes from the reasoning that, if an item is an expense, it is not possible to trace it to whatever is being costed. This is possible and occurs often but only in certain industries.

If an expense is incurred specifically for the job concerned and will not be used on any other, then it may be treated as a direct expense. For example to give a very simple situation, in contracting, the whole contract is often treated as one large job and it is easy to identify all the labour and materials used. Equipment bought for the contract is identified just as easily and if, when the contract terminates, this equipment is to be sold off and not merely moved on, it is a direct expense.

On the other hand if the equipment was to be used for several contracts, it would not be possible to allocate a precise cost to the particular contract, and the cost would have to be pro-portioned. Then it is an indirect expense.

Other examples are found in engineering when a special set of drawings need to be prepared for a specific job or there has to be a jig purchased, which, once the job is complete, will have no further use.

The total of the direct material, labour and expense is usually known as the PRIME COST (or more recently, the direct cost).

Indirect costs
Direct costs form a very substantial part of the cost of a product in most situations, but they cannot reflect the total cost. Other costs are necessary to bring the product or service from the prime cost stage to the point of sale to the customer. Some of these costs would be too expensive to identify and charge separately in their own right. Others need to be spread over several jobs and it is not possible to identify any portion with a particular job. Thirdly there are the costs which are a part of the general running of the business.

Once again they split down into the three categories of materials, labour and expenses. Collectively they are known as the OVERHEADS although for convenience and control it is usual to separate them as the factory (or production) overhead, the selling and distribution overhead and the administrative overhead.

Indirect materials usually cater for the items too small to be recorded when allocated. For example, in engineering cotton waste is often used to keep a piece of work clean. It is consumed on that piece of work and then discarded. It could be isolated as a cost but it is so small the cost of recording would be greater than the cost concerned.

In this case a quantity of cotton waste is drawn from the stores at the start of the work-shift, used as required, and the cost is spread across the jobs going through the cost centre in a fair manner.

Other items in a similar category would be seasoning in the catering industry or small split pins or fasteners in engineering.

Indirect wages would bring in the cost of supervisory wages where the manager concerned is looking after several production locations with different jobs going through each. To attempt to record the amount of time supervising each of the jobs would be counter-productive. It is far more satisfactory to record his total wage and then to spread this over each job on the basis of the time taken for each job to pass through the cost-centre concerned.

Another example would be in catering where the usual basis for a cost is the cost of a dish of a given number of portions. With the cooking and the serving staff dealing with a mixture of dishes during the course of the working day, it would be impossible to say how much of the chef's time went into preparing a bowl of soup.

Indirect expenses are usually gathered from all the other activities forming a part of the operation and must be recovered through the selling price if the business is to survive. They are allocated on the most convenient and fair basis and not all overheads are apportioned to the unit of production in the same manner. For example, the heating of a workplace could be apportioned according to the cubic capacity of the centre and then in relation to the work passing through.

This is not done in such an isolated manner as it seems. All the overheads would be collected for the centre and then, as a total, apportioned to the work passing through.

Other bases which can be used are: the number of employees at a cost centre; the value of the assets used in the centre; or the value of sales at a profit centre. Each situation will dictate its own requirements.

Unit of Production

The centre point of all cost collecting will be the unit of production and will be chosen as appropriate. It may be a component part, for example the cost per bolt manufactured. It might be the cost per operating passenger mile for a bus service or a train, the cost per ton-kilometre for an air-freighting service or per barrel of oil for a refinery.

The nature of the product or service will dictate the unit and there is nothing to prevent a production centre from finding the costs of different units of production. Very often as a part of a process several different products emerge which will have entirely different forms. It could be that one needs to be measured by the litre, another can have an individual identity as a piece, while a third is measured by the tonne. Some may be by-products of the main products or in other cases they could all be the main products or services.

Costing Methods

Modern thinking recognizes two methods of costing and all others are combinations and variations of the basic forms.

The two are JOB COSTING and PROCESS COSTING.

Job costing can be used when the unit of production can be isolated and the costs charged directly. For example, an engineering workshop undertakes the repair of machines and each machine is given a separate job number by which it can be identified.

At the other extreme is the process costing where the process is a homogeneous mass so each unit of production is indistinguishable from the next. A very good example is the oil refinery which usually takes a 'barrel' as the unit. While the oil is flowing through the process of refining one barrel cannot be distinguished from another.

Many production systems will be seen either to be a mixture of, or a variation on these.

Contract costing in the construction industry is job costing on a very large scale and the operating of an airline could be termed a form of process costing.

Batch costing is a combination form and is used when the treatment of each item of a production run of identical components as an individual job would not be economical although it would be possible. The economic batch is treated as one job but to find the cost of one, the total costs of the batch is divided by the number produced.

The need to divide a production run by the units produced is a feature of the costing of a process. While the result can be only an average, the correct siting of cost centres along the process line can give a satisfactory control of information.

Within both methods it is possible to have sub-jobs or sub-processes costed separately and when by-products need processing the isolation of these costs becomes important. On the other hand there are occasions when the start of the production can be a process in itself and the finished goods from this considered as the raw material for the next operation. This could be dealt with using a job-costing method.

No hard and fast rule can be given. The method to be used must be the choice of the management based as usual on their information needs.

Control

With the unit of production decided and the method of costing chosen, the next major step is to control the collection of the facts on the elements of cost. To allow the costs to be entered as the clerical staff think fit would defeat the whole purpose and so a system must be established.

The purpose is to follow the convention of consistency.

Control of materials

The main strut of the control of materials is to make certain that materials are not used without a record being made. In most organizations where goods are produced, the materials are kept in a store. This does not have to be a covered building but can be an open area. The most important feature is the controlled access, and no goods can be issued without an authority.

The precise nature of the authority differs from organization to organization. It may be a stores requisition note for the issue of each item or it may be a part of the job ticket which will travel with the work as it moves through the production process. In something like an oil refinery it could be the meter reading as the crude oil is pumped from the storage tank into the start of the refining process.

Not only does the control allow the storekeeper to be responsible for the safety of his stores and to stop unauthorized use of materials but it also allows the management to see how much material is used on a job. This will reveal spoilt work, the level of scrap and the level of wastage and whether this is from a part of the work process or from the inefficiencies of the operatives.

Much of this control is done by value, and the value at which materials are moved in and out of stores has a considerable part to play in the profit determination of the business and sometimes the pricing of the finished product.

Whichever method of stock valuation is used, two important points arise. Firstly no profit should be allowed into the valuation; overhead recovery is permitted but normally this is dealt with through the general overheads system. Secondly, the physical movement of stock must bear no relationship to the financial movements. At all times the physical movement should be on the basis of first-in, first-out, that is, all the old stock is issued before starting on the fresh.

This first-in, first-out system is probably the most used method of valuing the issues. Known as FIFO it is permitted by governments as a fair method. The governments' interest is, of course, in the control of taxation receipts.

An alternative method is to use the LIFO system – last-in, first-out – and the reasoning is that this reflects a value of the issues near to a present-day value and helps to relate a true cost. It can cause distortions as from the records it can appear as if some of the stock has been in the stores from the commencement of the business, and should this be the case when an emergency run-out of the material occurs, there can be some peculiar issue prices, especially during times of high inflation.

Probably the most satisfactory value to use in the costing system to reflect the true cost is a replacement value, which might be termed as the next-in, first-out, or NIFO. It would help the costing system to make sure the prices charged are at the correct level, but the cost of finding the new price from catalogues or waiting for the new delivery would incur excessive extra cost and delav.

Control of labour

In the control of labour there are two main purposes. The first to ensure that the correct charge is made to the correct work and the second to make sure that the worker works efficiently and does not spend too much of his time idle.

The latter is mainly a reflection of management efficiency but if there is a component of idle time or waiting time, the returns from the costing system can highlight any excess. By the introduction of a simple system of coding the time spent idle can be pinpointed to where the weakness occurs. It could be due to waiting for work to arrive from an earlier process, breakdowns of machinery or other reasons. Also, by the comparison of the time taken to complete the work task against the planned time, the efficiency level of the worker can be judged.

However the most important aspect of the costing of labour is to find the cost of the labour element in the job and this needs a system of time recording.

This usually starts at the factory gate with worker clocking in, but with a large production unit the clocks are likely to be situated at convenient points within the compound to avoid congestion.

The record given is more for labour control than cost control. It shows for insurance purposes if the worker is on the premises and highlights absence or lateness so the appropriate action can be taken. The gate clock card also allows the cost office to reconcile the individual work-record with time on premises to ensure all time is recorded during the working day.

Within the work-place there needs to be a control but the method must depend on the product. It may be that the chargehand will allocate the work and record the time spent by the worker on each job given. An alternative could be for the worker to maintain his own worksheet and for the chargehand to verify the entries.

It may be found suitable to mechanize the procedure with the worker using a clock machine to stamp a time card at the commencement and completion of each job.

Unfortunately the problem is not solved by merely recording the time spent and then being able to convert this into money terms. In modern production organization many of the workers are receiving some form of incentive bonus and this must be calculated and charged to the correct account.

A similar problem arises with the payment of overtime at enhanced rates. How this is charged depends upon whether the overtime is worked at the request of the customer, when it is a charge to the job, or whether it was for the benefit of the business. In the latter case the portion of the wage charge at the enhanced rate is taken as part of the production overhead and not a cost to the job.

In some industries, instead of the labour cost being calculated on a time basis, a fixed price is agreed between the management and the worker, but even then there is usually an upper time limit placed upon it and some method of time recording needs to be retained, if only to guide the rate-setting for the future.

Whichever system is adopted, an important factor must be the accuracy and honesty in recording the time. This involves both the worker and the management, as an incorrect charge will destroy the whole of the costing record for the job. It is not unknown for a chargehand to adjust the time taken on a particular job to make it look right but in so doing he invalidates the objective of maintaining the costing system.

Control of overheads

Most of the control of the overheads is carried on through a budgeting process which is on a section or departmental basis. A plan is made of the expected expenditure, the actual results are compared and the differences examined to discover why they have occurred.

Budgets and budgetary control will be mentioned later in this chapter and then examined in more detail in Chapter Thirteen.

With the overhead charges, if materials have to be issued from the stores there must still be the normal safeguards of properly made out requisitions. For the wages of the chargehands and ancillary workers some record needs to be maintained of their attendance at the work-place.

Costing Systems

As has been stated, costing is the historical recording of events in detail with the objective of finding the cost of the unit of production but, as it has evolved, different systems have been developed to emphasize certain facts for managerial control.

In the basic system the costs are allocated to the job. The costs which are not direct are then apportioned on a suitable basis until they have all been absorbed and the unit of production reflects the total cost. Then, in theory at least, by taking this cost from the sales price the profit for the organization can be found.

Since to wait for all the overhead charges to be submitted and allocated would turn the historic costs into pre-historic costs, the accepted practice is to estimate these for the accounting year and to charge them as a percentage of the direct wages, the job handled, or some other appropriate basis, as each job passes the cost centre. Any over- or under-recovery is dealt with through the profit and loss account although it will also be reflected in the percentage used for the following year.

Due to wide ranges of fluctuations in the recovery of the overhead it is found that the absorption system is not satisfactory for all purposes, even if it is the most widely used. Instead the system of marginal costing was devised.

Originally this was an aid to pricing but it has been adapted. It has limitations but these will be shown in a later chapter.

In this system only the direct costs are controlled on a job basis together with what are known as VARIABLE COSTS. These are costs which vary, although not in direct proportion with the volume of production. Then the amount remaining between the variable costs and the selling price is known as the CONTRIBUTION. From the contribution must come enough to cover the remaining costs, the FIXED COSTS (those fixed over the normal range of production and not affected by the volume) leaving any balance as profit.

The fixed costs are usually controlled by means of budgets and the subsequent comparison of the actual costs incurred.

A budgetary control system is usually run in conjunction with another system for the production aspects. Plans of the expected costs and revenues are built up and these act as the blueprint and target for operations in the forthcoming period, usually one financial year. The budgets are then divided into shorter periods of one month or four weeks to show the pattern of trade and to reflect any cyclical and seasonal influences.

Finally, after the event, the actual results are tabulated and compared with the budgets and any significant differences from the projection are analysed to see why they exist and to decide if a correction of the route being taken is needed to bring the course of the business back to the way previously agreed.

A feature of a budgetary control system is the use of the principle of management by exception. If the actual agrees with the budget, the item is ignored but if there is a difference it is examined. In this way time is not wasted and can be concentrated on correcting deviations.

Budgetary control is directed at the plans of the business and take into consideration what is *expected* to happen in the light of known and anticipated events in the next period. Useful as it is, it does not show what *should* happen. This is left to the system of STANDARD COSTING.

This is a system which is well suited to the production function where the costs can be synthesised at the planning stage. The cost of materials can be obtained from specifications and price lists and the labour charge constructed by timing how long the job should take under agreed circumstances and relating the wage rate of the grade of labour which should carry out the job. In this way, if the volume of production can be fixed, the performance for the whole year can be seen.

The advantage of standard costing is it has a systematic basis rather than being based, as in budgetary control, on the expectations of what might happen.

Any variations either above or below the standard are analysed and by combining these and studying the effect, the business can be controlled.

Finally, many of these systems are combined and tailored to

suit the needs of the business and, as the source information for both the financial and costing systems are usually the same, a further step can be taken to integrate the whole. At one time this was a costly process with a concentration of clerical labour but now with the increasing capability of the electronic devices, such as computers, to deal with the mass of details necessary and to interrelate it, such a scheme is likely to gain popularity again.

Limits of Costing

There are limits to the effectiveness of costing beyond the figures produced. All systems can only be as good as they are designed to be and as good as the people operating them allow.

Top management must be committed wholeheartedly to the ideas so they not only back up what is happening but are seen to use the presented results sensibly and not as a weapon to wield against the subordinates when plans do not materialize exactly as anticipated.

Lower down, the more junior management must be told what is expected of them before the event and then supplied with the results. In particular they should be made responsible for the costs they can control and not for the uncontrollable as well, although it is sometimes useful for them to give information on the uncontrollable as it can influence their decisions.

At the operative level the purpose of costing needs to be explained so that the operators can see the benefits of making accurate returns and of not trying to distort the results if they look wrong. Very often in misguided loyalty, an operative will distort, say, the labour time, although the variation was not of his making and by not revealing the difference properly the matter could move forward to put, in an extreme case, the whole of his living in jeopardy.

Provided these limitations are considered, a system of costing can have a significant effect on the profitability of the business but still one factor remains and that is time.

By its very nature a cost cannot be established until after the event and one of the benefits to be taken from a system is to be able to see when things are beginning to go wrong. The sooner the deviations are brought to light, the smaller will be the damage caused.

Time is of the very essence in reporting on the costs incurred and the late presentation of information is probably the greatest limitation which is imposed on the effectiveness of the whole system.

PART II Applying the Techniques

Chapter Seven

Understanding the Meaning of the Accounts

Each year companies must produce a set of final accounts constructed from the financial records. Usually there are two sets, one for internal use by the management, and the other, with less detail, for the use of the public.

By themselves they show a set of figures laid out in an orderly manner with so much as profit for the year, and the financial position carefully balanced so the sources of capital can be seen, with details of how it has been employed. As they are, they are worthless. The profit may look high but it may be only one-quarter of the profit made the year before. In the balance sheet all the amounts may be substantial but what has to be discovered is whether or not the assets are being used to their full capacity.

What is needed is for the accounts to be interpreted, for the meanings of the figures to be understood, the relationship between them to be explored and finally for a comparison to be made with other similar figures. This is necessary for the progress of the company to be judged.

The comparison is essential as, without it, there is nothing to show whether the accounts show a near disaster or satisfactory progress. It may be a comparison with the previous year, it may be with a comparable firm or, hopefully, where the internal accounts are concerned, it may be with the planned results.

The study in this chapter is to find the framework for interpretation to be adapted for various purposes.

Each reader of accounts will look for different aspects according to his needs. The investor will be looking at the performance to decide whether the company is performing satisfactorily or if he would be better to sell the shares and invest elsewhere. The banker will be looking at the security offered. The government tax official will be using them to check if the amount of tax collected is correct in relation to the performance.

Whatever the use, it is necessary to understand the meaning of the information supplied, to establish a relationship between the figures and finally interpret the trends. Beyond that point the different purpose will dictate further information to be extracted.

It is surprising how, by comparing the figures produced for a company with even those of the year before, facts not obviously visible become apparent.

What is Available

In the first part of this book the final accounts were constructed from the financial accounting records to the extent of the profit and loss account with a financial statement, the balance sheet.

The purpose of the profit and loss account was to analyse the rise or fall in the retained profit amount shown in the balance sheet and the amount of detail given was the choice of the management. This is a satisfactory arrangement for internal purposes but when there is the need to show the accounts to the external reader difficulties arise.

The management is usually reluctant to publish any facts at all; they fear their competitors will learn all the secrets and the weaknesses. If accounts are published without control then the public are at the mercy of the accountant who prepared them as to what has gone in and how it is expressed.

Unless this is known, meaningful interpretation becomes almost impossible.

In view of this constraint most countries impose obligations on companies to reveal certain details and, in some countries, the format of the accounts is made compulsory.

In the United Kingdom the law states that a limited liability company must publish once in each financial year, not only a balance sheet but also a profit and loss account, and if the company has subsidiaries (meaning that it owns over half the capital in other companies), it must produce a consolidated profit and loss account as well as the consolidated balance sheet so that the financial state of the 'whole family' of companies may be seen. The contents of the accounts are also stated and, to help supply information which is essential to judge progress but which cannot be expressed within the accounts, as for example, the number of employees, a report is made by the directors to the shareholders.

These accounts and the report supply much less information than the set available to the management but in the United Kingdom they must be sent to all shareholders, to all debenture holders and also be made available to the general public at selected government offices.

Unfortunately even with the compulsory disclosure there is no guarantee that similar items will mean the same thing in sets of accounts from two companies. Public accountants, when carrying out the audit of the final accounts, differ in their opinion on how the law should be stated and on the degree of disclosure.

This weakness was first dealt with in the United States of America by the setting up of an Accountancy Standards Board.

The Board issued a set of standards of practice over the years with the aim of ensuring that all sets of accounts published for corporations complied with the requirements. Power has been given to enforce compliance and the Securities Exchange Commission also monitors published accounts to ensure they are in accordance with the standards.

In the United Kingdom the accountancy professional bodies came together voluntarily to draw up a set of standards but, as the law was silent on how to enforce them, a novel solution was introduced pending the possible passing of legislation.

Under United Kingdom law, all limited liability companies must submit their final accounts for audit. The auditors they choose must be drawn from one of the professional accountancy bodies, authorized by the Companies Act to be auditors, and as those bodies were represented on the committee introducing the standards, compliance was easily enforced.

They instructed their members to advise their client companies to use the standards when making up their accounts. If they refused to do this the auditors were instructed to qualify the certificate given with the accounts. Then the shareholders and the other users would be able to see the degree of validity on the matters covered by the standards.

If the auditors themselves refused either to advise their clients to comply, or to qualify the auditor's report, they were liable to be removed from the membership. When they were removed from membership, they lost the right to audit the accounts and so compliance became complete.

The latest development in standards is for the accountancy bodies in all the major trading nations to come together to issue International Standards in the hope that it will eventually be possible to take a set of accounts from any of the countries concerned and to know that a certain term will have a particular meaning and the items making up the term will be the same irrespective of the country of origin. This will be of great assistance when attempting international interpretation.

Although the profit and loss account, as well as the balance sheet, has become compulsory and the contents standardized for many items, to obtain a reasonable view of the condition of the company some supplementary information is necessary.

A report from the directors has been mentioned and the modern practice for the company with a Stock Exchange quotation is to go even further. They issue a Statement of the SOURCES AND APPLICATION OF FUNDS (now made compulsory by requirements of a standard), an ADDED VALUE STATEMENT and often a statement to convert the profit from an historical basis to reflect current values (this has come about through the effects of inflation). Statistical information on the financial results over the last ten years is usually included, as well as a review by the chairman of the Board of Directors of the company's progress during the last year and sometimes giving his view of the future prospects.

The benefit of the Sources and Application of Funds Statement is to analyse the movement of funds in the company. The Profit and Loss Account is confined to the analysis of operating and does not cover capital items although it does contain some items which do not involve cash entering or leaving the business, such as depreciation. With these restrictions the disposal and the sources of the finance necessary to run the company, both for operating and for replacing assets, cannot be found from either the profit and loss account or the balance sheet and so this statement becomes essential.

The Added Value Statement is produced to show how the cash benefit from sales is dispersed. It shows how much is used to buy the materials and run the company, how much is used to pay the labour force, how much goes for taxation, how much is paid out to shareholders as dividend and how much is re-invested.

In some countries there is a further statement which is being introduced as a SOCIAL ACCOUNT to attempt to show how great is the impact of the company's activities on the environment and how much money the company is spending to combat the pollution it creates.

For really serious interpretation there is a need to go away from information supplied to the public by the company and to monitor both the financial and general press. Announcements of new orders and products indicate progress; advertisements for staff either show expansion or dissatisfaction through staff leaving. All these complete the picture together with the announcement of the price of the shares on the Stock Exchange which gives a valuation of the company in the eyes of the public.

Use of Accounting Ratios

All the sources of information to use when interpreting a set of accounts have been mentioned as well as the need to compare them.

Comparison will reveal the trend but, unless like is compared with like, it is of little use. For example, although there is more profit in cash terms, a company which makes £5,000 on sales of £15,000 is not performing as well as one which makes £4,000 on £10,000.

To achieve this similarity a common base must be found. This can be by expressing one figure as a percentage of another and then making a similar calculation for the comparative figure. Alternatively, a figure can be expressed as a ratio of another from the same year with, again, a similar calculation carried out on the comparative information. A third method is to calculate the number of days involved; for example the number of days the debtors are taking to pay compared with the time taken in a period twelve months earlier.

All three methods are included in the general term of ACCOUNTING RATIOS and it is these and not the absolute figures which make interpretation meaningful.

Limits to Interpretation

It must be realized that a set of final accounts cannot tell the full story of any business, bearing in mind one of the original concepts that only amounts and events which can be quantified can be reflected in them.

Even with the accepted additional British concept that the accounts should show a true and fair view of the affairs of the company there is still a scope for concealment. The reader has to be wary of such refinements as a change in the format from one year to another and must look into the reasons for the change.

Then comes the problems of the disclosure itself and the construction leading up to the figures. The fact that there has been compliance with the law does not mean the construction of those figures is entirely clear. With the coming of the accountancy standards of practice there is an ongoing improvement but unless the state is reached of a standardized bookkeeping system throughout the world, identical building up of amounts in the accounts must remain idealistic.

Finally, and again reverting to the concept of quantification, there cannot be a fully scientific basis for the interpretation of accounts. A great deal must be dependent upon instinct and 'reading between the lines', skills that will develop only by being aware of the legal, quasi-legal and other requirements plus a great deal of practice.

Chapter Eight

Fabric of the Accounts

The legal requirements are to some extent the scaffolding around which the published accounts are constructed. It is a minimum laid down and must vary from country to country.

Some countries base their requirements on what is thought best from the economic viewpoint, others on what is best for the administrative processes, whilst others may be simply bringing into the law what is already accepted commercial practice.

In Europe, the European Economic Community have enacted a series of directives to the member states instructing them to bring in a series of disclosure requirements with the view to producing a uniform scheme. Most of the requirements are found in the Fourth Directive on Company Law.

In turn, the individual countries must put the requirements of the directives into their own legal system by passing laws according to their usual procedures. At present, in the United Kingdom most of the requirements are to be found in the Companies Acts 1948 to 1976.

Below, the main requirements of the law are listed but, it must be emphasized, the law is in a constant state of change with more requirements being added either by further enactments or by the modern method of issuing regulations under an existing act and so being able to avoid the time-consuming full process of passing new legislation.

Balance Sheet

Share Capital
Both the authorized and the issued share capital needs to be shown and, for the issued, the amount paid up. The shares need to be classified under the various types.

Although the authorized capital must be shown it is not a part of the accounting needs of the balance sheet. It is the maximum legal limit up to which shares can be issued. Beyond that point certain formalities must be carried out by the shareholders and additional duty paid to the government.

The reason for its disclosure is to allow the investors and potential investors to discover how far the existing capital may be 'watered down'. Under the terms of most articles of association companies give their directors power to issue shares as they think fit up to the authorized limit. The issue may be for cash or for the exchange of shares or assets in another company but if the shares concerned are ordinary shares not only do the existing shareholders have an entitlement, should the company cease, to the nominal value of their shares but a proportion of the undistributed reserves of the company is theirs as well.

If further ordinary shares are issued then the reserves are spread not just amongst the earlier shareholders but with the new, as well. The result will be that the shares of the existing holders will drop in value as the market price takes into consideration the reserve entitlement of each share.

It is for this reason many companies on the Continent of Europe must either obtain the authority of the existing shareholders before issuing further shares or must first give them the opportunity to buy.

The need to show the issued and paid up capital is concerned with the security offered to the creditors. Under all company law systems the shareholder is the last to be paid in the event of all assets being sold off, and, if the creditor can see the share capital being used to finance assets, he knows under the terms of his security that he is entitled to be paid from those assets before the shareholder.

Other aids to the investor will include information on options to purchase shares at a prearranged price, usually below the current market price. These options may be in connection with an earlier transaction but are more likely to arise from the power of certain debenture holders to convert their loans into shares.

In recent years, options have arisen from the creation of incentive shares for senior employees.

The disclosure of options is necessary to show that the company is unlikely to be obtaining the full amount it could have obtained if the shares had been issued for cash on to the market.

Other information required on shares concerns redeemable preference shares, where they exist. Normally a company, when it has issued this type, cannot repurchase them unless they were issued with the power to be redeemed at some future date.

This becomes a contractual obligation and the disclosure is to allow those dealing with the company to be able to assess the consequences. The date of redemption must be shown and, to let the full liability be seen, the premium to be paid on redemption. Redemption can be carried out by financing from the proceeds of a new issue of shares of any chosen type or by the payment of cash generated by profit.

When this occurs an equivalent amount must be held as a capital reserve or the capital security in the company will be weakened.

It will seem obvious that all this information cannot be put into the body of the account, otherwise it would run on for pages. The modern approach is to show the main heading in the balance sheet or whichever account is being dealt with and to put all the detail into descriptive notes which are attached. In this case the balance sheet would have one figure for Share Capital, leaving the breakdown and other facts in the notes.

Reserves

These must be shown under the headings appropriate to the business and, in particular, the share premium reserve must be shown to the extent it has not been used for an authorized purpose, such as the issue of bonus (script issue) shares to existing shareholders.

As the reserves may be of a capital nature or brought in from revenue, care must be taken to distinguish between them. The revenue reserves come from the profits and, provided details are given, there is no reason why the directors should not decide to return them and then to distribute these past profits as dividend.

At this point a sub-total is normally taken to show the financial interest the shareholders have in the company. This figure is important as several accounting performance ratios are based upon it.

The remainder of the 'Sources of Capital' sector of the balance sheet is usually taken by the long-term liabilities and what is often called the 'Loan Capital'.

In strict legal terms 'capital' should be confined to the share capital but all languages change with time and this now refers to the money borrowed on a long-term basis either by a placing or, if the borrowing is very large, by an issue to the public.

Debentures are documents evidencing a loan and are not mentioned specifically in this part of the United Kingdom legislation. All references are to loans which are to be distinguished from bank loans and overdrafts. These other loans are to be subdivided between those repayable within the next five years (irrespective of when they were issued) and those repayable beyond that period. For all loans the security needs to be shown but not details of the asset forming security. The rate of interest must appear as well as the earliest date of redemption. From this the value of the security can be seen together with the interest burden and the financial pressure which will be brought about when the loans have to be repaid.

By showing the security the likely lender can see what security he can negotiate, if he decides to proceed.

With a loan there is no stipulation that it must be secured and for the large companies many of the recent issues for money raised both in the domestic market and overseas have been completely unsecured. The holders of these debentures or, for a public issue, the loan or debenture stock, have priority in the case of the loan needing to be repaid before its due date. This priority is only equal to that of the trade creditors.

For such a loan to take place the funds contributed by the shareholders must be substantial, and in assets such as in freehold properties, so the risk is not as great as it may appear.

Provisions
These must appear, if significant, and under this heading would come a pension fund provision where the company has,

under advice from the actuaries, built up a fund to meet an increasing liability on the company to pay pensions in the years ahead.

Provision for depreciation of the fixed assets is dealt with earlier and the provision for doubtful debts is normally deducted from the total of the debtors.

Amounts for deferred taxation, being a provision, are shown but the contents are now in accordance with an Accounting Standard. The effect of this standard is to include, in deferred taxation, only those amounts which are likely to have to be paid by the company to the taxation authorities at some time in the future.

Capital Employed

In the part of the balance sheet concerned with the capital employed there will appear details of the fixed and current assets, the investments, the intangibles and the current liabilities. How they are arranged will depend upon the management's choice and the need to highlight certain features.

Fixed Assets

These must show the cost or the valuation of the asset. The value may be as at the time the 1967 Companies Act came into force if the cost could not be found but it is far more likely to be when assets have been re-valued in an attempt to reflect the current values.

This revaluation is normally carried out for land and buildings and the year of valuation together with the name and qualifications of the valuer must appear. For assets, other than land and buildings, cost is the usual base and should there be any marked difference in value from the book value the directors will give an estimate to be shown as a note.

The fixed assets must be subdivided into groups suitable to the business and for each group show the amount of any disposals or additions. The accumulated depreciation must be shown for the final amount at the end of the accounting period.

If the fixed assets concerned are land (and buildings) there must be a further subdivision into freeholds, long leases and short leases.

Investment

There are some assets, to use the legal term, which are neither fixed nor current and investments are included in this group.

While details of the investments do not have to be shown they must be divided into the investments listed on a recognized stock exchange and those unlisted. Both are usually shown at cost and the listed securities must show the total market value at the date of the balance sheet by way of a note. This amount is found by looking up the closing price in a financial newspaper and simply multiplying by the holding.

Unlisted shares present a little more difficulty as, unless there has been a valuation during the recent past as for death duty purposes, the directors must give their opinion of the value. More often this is put as the cost value but as additional information the profits arising from the unlisted investments must be shown, if the holding is over 20%. More detail is required on the investments, if the interest is over 50%. Companies must list all their subsidiaries (unless the list would be too long, when only the principal subsidiaries need to be included in the published report). The name, percentage held and the country of registration is needed. If the holding is above 20% but below the 50% of a subsidiary then it is treated as an associated company and similar details shown.

This information is used in interpretation to analyse the result to see if the company is in fact an investment company, if it has made a series of useless investments or to monitor any major diversification of product.

Current assets

These are shown under the same headings as in the internal accounts: stock, debtors and cash.

Stock needs to be shown at cost or, if the directors consider the value to be significantly different, a note of the value needs to be shown. Work-in-progress is shown with the stock and the basis declared. At present there is no legal obligation to divide the stock and work-in progress although an accounting standard now sets out divisions.

As has been mentioned debtors are shown net of any provision.

If the accounts being considered are not those of a holding company, which must produce the consolidation, there may be an amount showing as owing to or from a subsidiary or fellow-subsidiary. When this appears the reader of the accounts needs to be aware of intergroup trading with the possibility of transactions not on the same basis as external dealings.

In the consolidated accounts the inter-group trading is eliminated as a sale to one company is recorded as a purchase at the same price by another within the group, thus cancelling out.

Current liabilities

These must be shown with amounts material and appropriate to the business of the company and, in particular, both the amount of the proposed dividend and the taxation due in the coming year, need to appear.

It should be noted, in the British accounts, the dividend can be the proposed amount only, although there may have been an interim paid out in the year. Directors can recommend only – it is for the shareholders to resolve at the annual general meeting whether or not to pay themselves.

At the meeting, the shareholders consider the accounts and, hopefully, approve them but unless the accounts are to be incomplete until after the meeting, as in some European countries, this amount is inserted. It is rare for the dividend not to be approved.

Goodwill, patents and trade marks

All these are shown at cost but there is no need for them to be split into three separate amounts. If the profits permit they are usually written off as soon as possible.

When interpreting the accounts it has to be remembered these are not tangible assets and often they must be deducted from the capital employed.

77

Preliminary expenses and share issue expenses

These come into the same category, and as they represent the spreading of a previous expenditure, do not form a true part of the capital employed in earning.

Contingent liabilities

Although not in the accounts the figure for contingent liabilities is very important when judging the financial situation. These are liabilities which have not yet been charged to the company but which are of material amounts and which could, when the charge is finally made, change the position. The law requires two categories to be brought in – where the contract has been placed but the work not completed or charged and where the directors have approved the expenditure but the orders have not yet been placed.

The purpose is to stop the abuse where the accounts are prepared to, say, 31 December in a year and the charge is put back to the middle of the following January. The amount, if included before, could have put the company in jeopardy.

There is also a provision to state the details, if any of the assets of the company have been pledged as a guarantee for the debts of a third party.

Comparative figures

These must be supplied for the balance sheet (and for the profit and loss account) and are the figures for the year before. If there has been a change in the base of the figures during the current year, the previous figures must be changed in a similar manner, as far as possible. Where it is not possible to change to the new basis, a note must be given to explain the effect.

Profit and Loss Account

Turnover

Turnover figures must be given if in excess of £250,000 per year, unless the business of the company specifically exempts this requirement. Banking is an example of this.

This turnover figure is shown more by way of a note although in the main body of the account, as when showing the profit and loss account to be published, no information is given as to the cost of sales. The account commences at the net profit in the internal accounts adjusted to reveal certain disclosures.

The turnover figure must, in the notes, be broken down over the main activities of the company and as far as possible the profit attributable to each activity shown. The turnover figure is essential when calculating some of the profitability and performance ratios.

Incoming rents

Certain other items of expenditure and revenue must be shown separately and the modern practice is to include the amounts within the profit figure and to show them as a note. Of the revenue, any rents received must be shown.

One purpose of this requirement is to bring to the notice of the reader any diverting of assets into property owning rather than other activities, if these were the aims of the company. It also allows the rents to be related to the property, to show if there is the correct return on investment being earned.

Income from investments

Another item in the revenue earned is income from investments. This must be divided to show the amounts from listed and unlisted investments.

Depreciation

Of the expenses, the depreciation for the year must be shown together with the amounts paid out of interest. As in the balance sheet the latter must be divided into the interest paid on bank loans, overdrafts and loans of similar nature with a short period, and the interest on other loans.

Remuneration

The remuneration of the auditors must be included as will be the directors' remuneration which will have to be divided to show the amount received by the chairman of the board of directors and the rest of the directors. This latter figure is shown by the numbers of directors with salaries put into bands of £2500. A similar analysis is needed for employees whose remuneration exceeds £10,000 per annum.

Outgoing rents

If it is material, the amount charged for the rent of plant and machinery must be shown. At first sight this may appear to be a frivolous requirement but in fact it is most important when examining the burden of fixed interest charges.

Should a company fail to pay the interest on a loan the usual procedure is for the lender to realize the security and to use the proceeds to pay back the principal sum lent and the arrears of interest. Should the company have a heavy charge for rent and fails to pay, then the owner will repossess. In either case the company could be deprived of production and other facilities as well as the ability to generate revenue.

By adding together the interest and the rental charges the amount which must be earned can be seen clearly.

Extra-ordinary items

If any charge or credit arises from an event in previous years this must be shown separately as must extraordinary items which have occurred outside the normal trading activity of the company. Within this category would be a material profit made on the sale of an asset, if this was not to be treated as a capital receipt, or a large profit or loss incurred on a foreign exchange transaction.

Beyond this point the requirements are concerned with showing the appropriation of the profit rather than the earning of revenues.

Corporation tax

The charge for corporation tax must be shown with some note as to the basis and details of any relief from double taxation when some of the profits have also been taxed in a foreign country.

Reserves and provisions
Amounts moved in and out of reserves and provisions must appear with any amounts put by for the redemption of shares or debentures.

Dividends
Finally, any dividends paid or recommended from the profits of the year need to appear and the amount remaining is the retained profit.

Directors' Report

The information which must go into the directors' report will be in two categories, the items only indirectly of use in assessing a company and the rest which can be used directly to advantage.

General information
In the first category will be the names of persons who are or who have been directors during the year, together with details of their shareholdings in the company and also the holdings of their immediate family where there is a beneficial interest. Contracts entered into by the directors, in which the company has an interest, must be mentioned.

Other general information to be shown include political and charitable donations if in excess of £50 in the year and if the company has to show the turnover, the amount of the exports in that figure.

Activities and any changes
Items which will be of direct use will be the activities and any changes in the year, if significant. Any significant changes in the fixed assets and, if the assets changing include land, any material difference in the value from the cost or valuation figure with a comment from the directors on the accuracy of their estimation, must appear.

Issue of shares
An issue of shares or debentures calls for comment with details of the reason for the issue, the size, the class of security issued

and the consideration that the company received. This information is useful when calculating the performance of extra investment.

Turnover and profit and loss
Details of the classified turnover together with the profit and loss for each activity need to be shown.

Weekly average number of employees
This must be shown with the total of their remuneration. Although this figure was first introduced to enable a check on whether fair wages were being paid it becomes of use to the interpreter to see the earning capacity and the performance of the labour force.

Statements of Standard Accounting Practice

As all accounts are considered to involve some element of judgement and no two accountants will produce an exactly identical set of accounts from the same basic information, an ever growing flow of accounting standards is being issued by the accountancy controlling associations throughout the world in an attempt to achieve uniformity.

In the United Kingdom some of the main standards cover the items below but it must be emphasized that with new standards being issued either in final or discussion form every month or two, this list cannot be exclusive and needs to be brought up-to-date continuously.

Associated companies
The first standard was to cover the treatment of associated companies in the profits. These are companies in which the shares held are not more than 50%, so it is not a subsidiary with the need for consolidation of the accounts, but more than 20%, so the profits could have a marked effect.

With an interest of over 20% the investing company can exercise a great deal of influence. As this influence will probably be reflected in the profits it is considered to be right for a part of the profits of the associate to be included in the results of the investing company, whether or not they have been distributed as dividend.

The theoretical idea is that the shareholders in the investing company can then see how well the total capital employed in their company is performing.

If the investing company is a holding company, the profit share, in proportion to the holding of ordinary shares, will be brought into the consolidated profit and loss account and, to give the required balance in the financial statement, the cost of the investment in the associate will be increased by the amount the share of the profit exceeds the dividends received from that investment.

If the investing company is not a holding company, the share of profit is put into the profit and loss account only.

Disclosure of accounting policies

This is the subject of the second standard and is used if the accountant believes he is departing from the use of the concepts of going-concern and accruals or the conventions of consistency and prudence. Policies must be disclosed, also, when the items concerned are judged to be material or critical.

For example, policies could be stated for debtors and likely bad debts, depreciation and calculation of turnover.

As they show the basis of the amounts, they are essential reading for the user of the accounts.

Calculation for earnings per share

These are in the third standard and concern a very important ratio used for listed companies when examining performance from the investors' viewpoint or in calculating a market valuation of the shares.

A problem in the past has been in deciding the amount to be put into the earnings; should it be before or after taxation, should it be after the preference dividend? There are many more variations which can be introduced.

The standard has now specified the items to be brought in so that when comparing the earnings ratio from one company to another the same basis will be used.

To understand the full detail or to construct a set of accounts to comply with the standard, it is necessary to consult the document. For the purpose of interpreting, the elementary theory will be sufficient. In calculating the profit to be used the figure to be achieved is that of the earnings of the shareholder arising from trading in the year. For this the profit is taken after taxation, minority interests if the company is a holding company, and preference dividends.

Extraordinary items and previous year items are ignored, whether they are gains or losses.

To obtain the number of shares to complete the ratio the criterion is the number of ordinary shares issued at the end of the period and entitled to dividend.

Government grants
Standard four is for the treatment of government grants and how they should be related to the expenditure.

Two methods are permitted. The amount of the grant can be deducted from the cost of the asset for which it was paid and the balance of cost depreciated in the normal manner, or the amount of the grant can be held as deferred income and an amount credited to profit and loss each year over the life of the asset.

In the second method care must be taken to ensure the 'deferred income' is kept away from the shareholders' funds.

Value added tax
This and its treatment in accounts became standard five.

Basically, unless the tax charged to the company is not recoverable it is excluded from all calculations and it is also ignored when the turnover is stated.

With the debtor or creditor for VAT, which must occur as the Customs and Excise are paid quarterly, this does not need to be shown separately.

As an alternative it is permitted to show the turnover including the VAT provided the amount of the VAT is disclosed.

Extraordinary items and prior year adjustments
These are covered in standard six and have been mentioned earlier when the contents of the profit and loss account were dealt with.

The underlying idea is to make sure all items affecting profit and loss are brought to the attention of the readers of accounts and, as far as possible, all the realized profits pass through, even if the amount of the profit is taken out again by a transfer to the reserves.

Also shown in this category are abnormal items; for example, where there has been an abnormal loss from some trading activity during the year, such as an exceptional loss in the value of stock, and it is felt that it should be brought to the attention of the shareholders.

Inflation

Standard seven was concerned with the adjustment of the accounts to reflect the effects of inflation but was withdrawn when the United Kingdom government decided to adopt a different method of dealing with the problem.

Taxation

The treatment of taxation in accounts has become somewhat confused involving three standards, eight, eleven and fifteen, one of which, eleven, had to be withdrawn when it was in conflict with some revised thinking by the accountancy committee devising the standards.

Standard eight is technical and achieves its objective in enabling the items to be dealt with in a similar manner. It involves mainly advance corporation tax under the imputed system of taxation and deals with how to show the tax due and how to treat the advance portion until it can be recovered.

Standard fifteen looks at the problem of deferred taxation and the effect is that the deferred taxation mentioned in the balance sheet will include amounts which are likely to be paid to the authorities at some time in the future and no amounts which were previously included to spread the effect of tax allowances and reliefs.

This standard has an influence on the interpretation as it means that when examining the long-term liabilities to see if further credit can be given, judgement is not blurred by the inclusion of fictitious liabilities.

Stocks and work-in-progress

These are catered for in standard nine and the accountant preparing the accounts is able to define the meaning of cost and the basis of valuation which should be used.

One of the main impacts arises from guidelines in the valuation of work-in-progress on long-term contracts where in the past it has been permissible to take the profit at the end only. Now, if the contract is reasonably advanced to the extent of twenty-five or thirty per cent it is permissible to take up two thirds of the profit earned to that stage, after allowing for known costs. This makes the profit and loss accounts for the years during which the contracts are being carried out show a more realistic figure and does not put an abnormal profit into the year of completion. It also means the work-in-progress figure in the balance sheet will not be inflated, although it is recommended that details are given of the gross valuation of the contract and of the progress payments received so the size may be judged.

Statements of source and application of funds

The 'flow of funds' statement as it is often called is the subject of standard ten. It will be dealt with in more detail later in this book but at this stage it is sufficient to state it looks at the use of funds in a business and attempts to show how they were derived, whether generated by trading or from other activities.

The law is silent on the need to provide the flow of funds statement but the accountancy profession have considered, quite rightly, that it is essential for the understanding of the financial position and have forced companies to publish it each year with their final accounts.

Depreciation

This is dealt with in standard twelve (standard eleven was withdrawn) and attempts to state what is depreciated rather than to control how an asset is to be depreciated. Depreciation is defined as 'the measure of the wearing out, consumption or other loss of value of a fixed asset whether arising from use, effluxion of time or obsolescence through technology and market changes'.

All assets which have a finite life must now be depreciated and this includes freehold buildings although the land on which they stand is still considered to be interminable and is not depreciated.

This standard does cause problems in property companies where there is a regular revaluation due to the influence of inflation but this may be eased when a standard can be devised on inflation accounting.

The method of calculating depreciation is not needed for this standard but should be shown as required by standard two on 'accounting policies'.

Research and development

Standard thirteen on the accounting for research and development is the result of many years of thinking and re-thinking by accountants.

The difficulty is found when considering whether any expenditure should be carried forward to future years when the benefit of the research is hoped to come to fruition. This is fraught with danger for there are many examples of this being done and when the project came to the market it was not a success. As a result the expenditure carried forward had to be written off against the profit in the disaster year when the company was not able to stand the strain.

In one famous example, this carrying forward of the charge was sufficient to conceal a lack of profitability and liquidity, resulting in a spectacular liquidation.

The rule, now introduced, is that expenditure on research and development should be set against profits in the year in which it is incurred. The reasoning behind this is that the company should be undertaking the research just to maintain its present position in its trade, and as the future benefits cannot be quantified properly it is impossible to state the correct amount to carry forward.

Research in this context has been given three meanings; pure research when the purpose is to gain technical knowledge and not to investigate a specific application; applied research where there is a specific application; and development which is to produce new products prior to commercial production.

Development is the only one of the three from which the expenditure may be carried forward to another year and then only under strictly controlled circumstances. It must be considered as deferred expenditure and not as an intangible asset to be amortized.

Conclusion

With the contents of the accounts now shown and the methods of application revealed from the standards, the reader of the accounts is now in a position to start to interrelate some of the figures by the ratios and to understand the meaning of the movements.

Chapter Nine

Using the Ratios

The first matter to consider when interpreting a set of accounts is the final objective. This determines the approach and the choice of the ratios to be used.

Then, after the approach and required end result have been decided, the information must be extracted systematically and finally brought together to assess the position. This is essential as many of the ratios are linked and the reason for a particular movement can be revealed through another sympathetic variation.

A study of the trends is essential. Where it is possible, the trend for five or even ten years will be useful but when doing this it is often necessary to look beyond the figures in a set of accounts. There is a need to study other facts such as a further injection of capital, a change of activity and even major changes in the management.

Ratios which are generally used are grouped in four convenient areas – those covering the liquidity of the business, its ability to pay the bills when they fall due; the ratios relating to the performance and including the profitability ratios; the ratios on the structure as this has a bearing on the security of loans and the availability of finance; and lastly, the financial ratios which look at performance and structure from the viewpoint of the investor and the financial markets. These are used to obtain the market value of the company in certain situations.

Liquidity Ratios

Two ratios dominate this sector, the CURRENT RATIO and the QUICK RATIO or ACID TEST as it is sometimes known.

Both use the working capital and show the relationship between the current assets and the current liabilities.

The current ratio

This takes an overall look at the ability to pay the debts due without having to sell some of the fixed assets. It is found by dividing the current assets by the current liabilities or to express this more precisely:

$$\frac{\text{Stocks} + \text{Debtors} + \text{Cash}}{\text{Current liabilities}}$$

Whether any overdraft is included in the current liabilities is a matter of choice but it can be argued that it should be excluded on the ground that this is a method of financing.

A movement downwards towards one (parity) and possibly below indicates a worsening of liquidity but a drop below parity often means approaching doom.

This will depend upon the industry concerned, the type of activity and the traditional levels. Before fixing a desired level, comparison needs to be made with other similar companies.

The disadvantage with the current ratio is the inclusion of stock. The aim is to see the ability to pay but the stock, although it can be realized in the long-term, cannot be easily sold. The value showing in the accounts is a value in use, the cost price. If the company were to try to sell it in another manner the chance of obtaining the book price would be small. As the company is in the market to buy rather than to sell the material concerned, it might be lucky to raise ten per cent.

A similar argument could be put forward for the debtors but it is felt that these are more easily matched to the creditors. As the cash comes in from the debtors, even if slowly, it is likely that the demands from the creditors will come in at the same speed.

The quick ratio

The ratio produced is the quick ratio or the acid test. It shows how the short term creditors can be paid out of the short-term debtors, with cash and near cash. Debtors are counted as all being good or the company would not have sold to them in the first place. The ratio is found:

$$\frac{\text{Debtors} + \text{Cash (or near cash)}}{\text{Current liabilities}}$$

Ideally this ratio should not fall below one but in some industries where long credit periods are traditional, it may fall as low as 0.5 without danger.

Should the company be trading in such a manner that it has a low level of creditors and no debtors or with an absence of debtors as it sells on a cash basis, the ratio will be distorted. In the financial company sector, it will be almost useless as an indicator, and more can be found by relating the working capital to the total assets.

Other liquidity ratios

To be able to pay the creditors a flow of cash needs to arrive in from the debtors and to check the success of a good credit control policy the debtors' period is calculated. Internally this should be done each month and allied to an aged debtors schedule to see where the laggards are to be found.

This is an average figure and is expressed as the number of days the debts are outstanding. The formula is:

$$\frac{\text{Closing debtors}}{\text{Total sales} \div 365} = \text{Credit period in days}$$

If the trend is upwards it may be a poor credit control or it may be the effect of a sales expansion and having to sell to customers not as creditworthy as could be desired.

It is unlikely that the figure will be below fifty days in the United Kingdom as the standard terms of trade are: cash on 30th of the month following date of invoice. This gives an average of forty-two days. Also, it shows the need to discover the customary credit period for the activity concerned. If it were found to be fifty days for a food supermarket company, there would be cause for alarm.

A similar calculation can be carried out for the creditors, although this is more accurate with access to the purchases in the internal accounts. However, a trend figure may be found by relating the creditors to the sales. Its importance is to see if the company is coming under increasing pressure from the creditors, a feature which normally occurs as the cash becomes short.

A further ratio which can be taken into this section is the ratio of:

$$\frac{\text{Working capital}}{\text{Total net assets}} \times 100.$$

This shows the stability of the company as the maintenance of sufficient working capital is just as important as providing the fixed assets.

With these ratios it is important to remember they need to be taken from the published accounts prepared on an annual basis and the results may be distorted by cosmetic reporting. A company can choose the timing of its year end to present the most satisfactory position in the year. For example, a departmental store will choose a time, probably at the end of January when the stocks have been depleted by the winter sales and the new stock for the following season has not been delivered. Stocks will be down, creditors will be down and cash will be up, producing a very favourable current ratio.

On the other hand an apparently poor position could be caused by the company's being poised for a sales expansion just into the year, but allied to that it is possible for certain stocks to be held back at the suppliers until after the end of the financial year (with delivery due in the first week of the next year). The balance sheet will appear satisfactory but, in fact, is worthless.

Performance Ratios

The basic ratios on performance are found by taking the GROSS PROFIT and NET PROFIT as a percentage of the sales.

Both are meaningful as internal aids. The gross margin shows the skill in trading and ensures that the correct margin is being added to the cost of sales to make the business profitable.

The net profit margin by itself is not a revealing indicator other than to show the percentage profit after allowing for the total costs. It can have a subsidiary use to monitor the administration.

If the difference is found between the net and gross margins, this figure is the percentage attributable to administration. If the gross margin is static or even improved but the net has fallen, then the fault is within the administration and a deeper probe can begin by subdividing the percentage breakdown into various headings, for example, selling, distribution, financial, etc.

As the sales and the production costs are closely related a far more reliable guide to the performance is to take the RETURN ON CAPITAL EMPLOYED. This will show whether the use of total assets is producing the required level of profit. In its basic form it is produced by:

$$\frac{\text{Net profit before tax}}{\text{Total net assets}} \times 100.$$

There are difficulties as there must be no doubt about which amounts are put into the numerator and which into the denominator. Some controversy exists as to whether the net profit should be before or after the interest and the dividend on the preference shares. Provided a consistent policy is followed the interpreter should follow the course to give him a result he can understand.

Sometimes the return is taken as the net profit to the equity investment but this becomes more of a financial ratio that would interest the shareholders.

The return on investment used to be a very popular ratio but this has now lost considerable favour other than when monitoring an investment using the capital appraisal techniques.

To monitor the use of the fixed assets, the following ratio is used:

$$\frac{\text{Sales}}{\text{Fixed assets}}$$

This will give the value of sales generated per £ of fixed assets and by dividing the sales by the number of employees the earning capacity per employee is produced.

Another indicator of performance is the STOCK TURN or

the average of the number of times the stock is replaced during the financial period.

The reason for this is simple – profit is earned only when the goods are sold to the customer, so the more frequently the stock has to be replaced, the greater must be the sales and hopefully the greater the profit.

To find the correct figure has its difficulties. In the first place unless there is access to the internal accounts and the amount of the purchases, an element of profit confuses the issue. But as this world cannot be perfect, when using the published accounts, a compromise must be accepted by using the sales as a base.

The second difficulty is caused by inflation. Unless some adjustment is made for inflation the stock figure in times of rising inflation will make it appear as if there is a slower turn round.

The ratio is found by:

$$\frac{\text{Sales}}{\text{Average stock for the year}}$$

The higher the number the more satisfactory will be the situation.

The figure for the average stock is found by the average of the closing stock from the balance sheet, and the opening stock which always shows as the closing stock in the comparative figures of the previous year.

Structure Ratios

These show the strength of the company from the type of investment and the relationship of funds from shareholders and funds from the various classes of lender.

By far the most important is the GEARING, the relationship between the equity and the fixed interest loans. This will be discussed in detail later but for this purpose it is enough to say that it shows the burden of the fixed charges and the risks taken by the holders of the equity shares (these are normally the ordinary shares as they obtain a repayment plus the share of any surplus).

The accepted level of gearing in the United Kingdom is one but with the added stipulation that the interest charge should be covered five or six times by the earnings in a year.

Another ratio in this sector is:

$$\frac{\text{Equity}}{\text{Fixed assets}}$$

It shows the extent of the investment by the shareholders and when compared with:

$$\frac{\text{Equity}}{\text{Total net assets}}$$

the proportion can be easily seen.

It means that the proportion not financed out of the equity must come from elsewhere and it must be loan capital.

The accepted practice is for the fixed assets to be financed from equity and hopefully a part of the working capital as well, with the balance coming from the loans. If the loan capital has to finance the fixed assets there is a chance of being 'locked in' and should it be necessary to release the sum lent, it might be difficult.

The fact that the fixed assets are offered as security for a loan, has no influenece on the purpose of the loan.

These ratios are used when further finance is needed to see if any loans can be made without a further issue of equity. This will be discussed later when examining the sources of finance together with the application of the financial ratios which have the purpose of assisting investors to make decisions.

Other Ratios

There are many other ratios, some main and others subdivisions for detailed examination of a particular section. Some will be dealt with in connection with other aspects of accounting but the reader and interpreter of accounts should try to seek out his own relationships.

Relate one item in the accounts to another and test whether it is meaningful, whether it tells anything about the business and gradually a series of effective ratios can be built up. Ratios which assist one interpreter will be discarded by another.

Chapter Ten

Absorption Costing

The most common method of costing used is the absorption method. This is probably because it is the easiest of the systems to use and understand, although the results are not the most scientific.

Much of the use is in the small businesses where extreme accuracy must be balanced against the cost of recording. It is a method which can be readily understood and for that reason, if for no other, its application will be continued for many years to come.

Theory

For the business to come into a profit situation, all the costs, no matter where they arise, must be covered and the selling price of the product must be sufficient to provide the chosen amount of profit. If the unit of production can be shown to cover all the costs than by simply adding the profit percentage, the price is reached.

By calculating the cost per unit, first for the direct costs and then apportioning the overheads, the total cost will be achieved.

Used for cost control this is a rough method but used for pricing it may mean some profits are being lost to the business. It is by far the best practice to charge what the market will bear and then to make sure the price fixed will enable the total costs to be covered.

In this way the profit obtainable for different markets or different groups of customers can be obtained.

The Practice

All the direct costs for materials, labour and expenses are gathered together and allocated to the unit of production. If a job costing system is being used this is a recording operation, but if batch or process production is needed the unit cost is a matter of dividing the appropriate costs by the number of units produced.

It may be more satisfactory for control purposes to put the direct cost collection through cost centres first but the result will be the same. For each unit there will be a cost of any materials, labour and expenses.

The problems will come in making a charge to each unit to cover all the other expenses in operating the business – the overhead charge.

By its nature it cannot be identified with a particular unit but it is just as much a cost as a direct cost. Some means have to be found to spread this in a manner which is not only fair but also tries to reflect the current situation.

In the average very small business a rough and ready method is used. The overhead costs for the previous year are taken, probably increased for the likely effect of inflation in the following year then expressed as a percentage of the wages. For quotation purposes this becomes the basic formula and the direct costs are found by recording in the normal way.

Of course, by using a percentage of the labour cost, it assumes the labour content will remain constant. It does not take into consideration what will happen if there is a fall off in sales with a resultant drop in production, or cater for a boom in sales with the higher expenditure on labour and materials.

This method will lead to massive over-recovery or under-recovery of the overheads but as most businesses of this size, regrettably, look only at the profit showing in the financial accounts to monitor progress, they do not feel affected.

With absorption costing, the over- or under-recovery is a feature and a weakness, for unless the output for the following year as well as the expenses, can be foreseen with accuracy, it must always be present.

To some extent, in the larger business, this can be mitigated by a much closer system of allocation using cost centres and differing appropriation to the centres for various types of expenditure.

Problems will arise in grouping expenses as many businesses have services that apply to several departments. For example, a repair workshop may be operated or a team of toolmakers work for a whole engineering process. Then there are the welfare services within the business and, finally, all the selling and administration departments. For a full system of absorption costing, all of these need to be brought in.

In practice, the procedure is to divide the expenses into those concerning the production unit, that is the factory or the workshop, and those others which are found outside that sphere of activity.

Method of allocating

All cost centres are designated either as production centres or as service centres and any costs which are solely for the centre concerned are allocated to it.

There are some expenses which are to the benefit of all or some of the centres and these are the next to be spread, and according to the nature of the expenses different methods are needed. The aim is to be fair, as far as is possible, and to make the spread within bounds of incurring extra expenses.

Some examples of the bases which can be used for common expenses are given. More exist and may be peculiar to a certain business. Also, it may be that for reasons of custom some businesses will use a different basis and there is no reason why this should not be so, provided the use is consistent and acceptable to the management.

Rent and rates: use the square area occupied.

Lighting: the square area occupied.

Heating: the cubic area occupied.

Power: either meter to the cost centre, base on the rating of the machine or tool or on a machine hour rate.

Welfare services: on the number of employees in each centre, although it is likely these charges may first be gathered in a service centre.

Depreciation: on the value of the assets in each centre.

Once all the costs have been allocated to a centre, the second stage is to isolate the service centres. Rank them in the order commencing with the service centre which serves most other centres, service and production.

Then allocate all the costs at that centre across all the others served by it using a fair method. If it is the repair department, for example, records would have been kept of the work done and the allocation could be a proportion based on the time spent in each department.

When the first centre has been eliminated, work down through the next in the order of service and so on until all the service centres have been eliminated and all the overheads relating to the factory are concentrated into the production cost centres.

The third stage will be to allocate cost, at production cost centre level, to each job or unit passing through the centre. This can be done by charging an amount per hour based on either the machine hours in the centre or labour hours worked in the centre. As an alternative an amount related to the value of materials passing through or related to the whole of the direct costs is used. A fair allocation is likely to differ from centre to centre.

Often, to save complications, the charge may be based on one of the factors and the most popular one is the labour cost, on the grounds this is usually common to all centres.

A difficulty arises as such a system of allocating costs is an historical one and to wait until all costs are in at the various centres would mean delays. The delays would probably be so long that the figures would be useless by the time they were presented.

To overcome this, estimates are made before the start of the financial year and these are related through the system down to the cost centres. To charge them to the job or unit is done by charging an amount in money per hour or, as is more likely, by charging a percentage of the value of one of the elements of the direct cost.

As there are two variable factors the level of production and the level of expenses – it will be impossible for the recovery of the expenses against the work passing through to be exactly as planned. There must be an over- or under-recovery.

To deal with this, the usual practice is to write off the difference to the costing profit and loss account and bring the costing records in line with the manufacturing account.

To make this write-off is more satisfactory than trying to adjust in the recovery percentages for the following year. The main reason is that the recovery percentage being used is linked (or should be linked) to the planned performance, and what is in the past has happened and cannot be changed.

This is not to say the past should be ignored, as many of the estimates may have been wrong by a large margin. These differences should be examined and if it can be seen that there are areas which can be rectified for the future these adjustments should be made.

Selling and administrative overhead

Once the factory overheads have been allocated the selling and administrative costs are charged to the product although this is not usually done by going back to the cost centres.

The costs concerned are usually collected on a departmental basis in order to keep some control.

They are gathered to be charged as a percentage based on either the factory cost, the labour element, the direct costs or some other suitable basis. It may be that there is a separate amount charged for the administration and for the selling or there may even be different amounts within one of the groups.

For example, it may be decided to charge different amounts for exports and domestic sales.

Conclusion

For a general overall control and for ensuring that the selling price covers the total cost a system of absorption costing will probably be sufficient.

By charging out to the unit of production, the amount of profit present in each unit can be easily seen and the more distinct each job becomes, as opposed to a process, the greater will be the value of this type of costing.

Even with its limitations it should not be discarded as useless and superseded by one of the later methods. In practice it is rare to find a business of any size which relies entirely on one costing system as it has to use the best from each with the aim of providing the organization with the information it needs to make decisions.

While absorption costing has defects when costing the production facilities and ensuring that they are performing effectively and efficiently, it is very sound for seeing the profit per unit.

It may not be the best to help with the recovery of overheads when looking at the business as a whole and making pricing decisions but it does monitor the correct margins. Linked with a budgetary control system, it can be used along with a system to collect the costs for selling and administration and to see the effect of this on the selling price and profit.

Lastly, as already mentioned, due to the simplicity which can be introduced and to the ease of understanding of the method, it is probably the best for the small business.

Chapter Eleven

Marginal Costing

Due to the deficiencies in absorption costing, new methods have been devised and one of these is marginal costing with its apparent roots in economics.

In economics the marginal cost is the cost of producing the extra unit, the one at the margin or on the outer limit. It is the same in costing, the cost of producing a unit is what matters.

The approach is to divide all costs into two groups, the variable costs and the fixed costs.

The variable costs are those that vary with the volume of production, although not necessarily in direct proportion. The fixed costs are those that remain static over the normal range of production.

In stating that the fixed costs remain static, this does not imply they never vary but that they are not linked to the production volume. Also, it is important to note that these are fixed costs and not the shut down costs.

SHUT DOWN COSTS refer to the expense of keeping a business on a 'care and maintenance' basis without any production but still in existence. Fixed costs apply where there is some production and the theory is that those costs will remain fixed whether the production is at a minimum or at the capacity of the facilities.

Some costs fall into the category of semi-variable, in that they show characteristics of both fixed and variable costs. They are normally of the type where there is an element of fixed charge which is payable whether or not any benefit is taken plus a charge based on consumption. A United Kingdom telephone charge falls into this group with a fixed charge for the rental of the equipment and a charge for the call units used in the period covered by the account.

When operating a marginal costing system these semi-variables cannot exist and the charges must be broken down into the fixed and variable elements.

The concept of marginal costing is that the fixed costs are an established fact so the control must be through the variables. Any difference between the variable cost and the selling price can only be a contribution to cover the fixed costs and to leave any remainder as profit.

Contribution

This idea of contribution can be understood by building up the price of a unit of production. Each Selling Price(S) is made up of Total Cost(T) plus Profit(P) or put another way:

$$S = T + P$$

Total cost is itself made up of the Variable Costs (V) plus the Fixed Costs(F) and the formula now becomes:

$$S = V + F + P$$

But it has been agreed the fixed costs and the profit are termed the Contribution(C) and the formula is:

$$S = V + C$$

This can be arranged to show:

$$C = S - V \text{ or}$$
$$V = S - C$$

Whichever way it is expressed it shows that if the variable costs are covered, the surplus must contribute to covering the fixed costs first and then the profit.

Control System

If marginal costing is used as a control then it is the variables that are monitored and kept as low as possible to allow the greatest contribution.

In practice, as a control system, marginal costing by itself has not been able to provide the answer but in the planning and pricing functions it remains established.

Use in Planning

One of the normally accepted objectives of a company is to make a profit and the planning function is, obviously, to achieve that goal.

To reach this goal it is useful to know the starting point where the profit is non existent but all the costs are covered. This is known as the break-even point (B/E) which is expressed as

$$B/E = V + F$$

and as the fixed costs are static any contribution beyond the break-even point is profit. A study of this profit is a study of the units at the margin.

Given the level of the fixed costs, it is a simple matter to calculate both the break-even point and the profit for any level of production.

Unfortunately, in planning, the question is often posed on the profit at a certain level of production and each time this is asked there has to be a separate calculation.

The other practical point is that, although the theory states that the fixed costs are static, in practice they vary within limits for the level of production. Many of the 'fixed' costs are in fact of a 'stepped' nature. They are static over a certain range and then rise sharply to remain static again over another similar range. For example, the chargehand in a factory may be considered to be a fixed cost. With a certain number of men and machines he can cope, but when production exceeds a certain level an extra chargehand must be employed, so the fixed cost rises sharply and will remain at that new level until the third chargehand is needed.

This will mean considerable calculation when planning with several alternative levels and by the time the planning team have sorted out the figures they want, time would have been wasted. In addition to the time wasting, many managers find they are not able to conceive an idea from figures and need a pictorial approach.

A break-even chart is constructed to show the situation.

However, before discussing both the construction and the meaning of the chart, one major limitation must be noted. As with any chart of this nature the degree of accuracy is restricted and a degree of tolerance has to be built in to a discussion. If this is recognized any accurate determination of either the chosen level or the break-even point can be found by calculation. It then acts as a check on the accuracy of the chart.

The formula for finding the break-even point is:

$$\text{B/E} = \frac{\text{Fixed costs}}{\underset{\text{(per unit)}}{\text{Selling price}} - \underset{\text{(per unit)}}{\text{Variable costs}}}$$

$$\text{or B/E} = \frac{\text{Total F}}{\text{S} - \text{V}}$$

The result will appear as a number of units of production.

In the first of the charts the cost and revenue expressed as an amount is put on the vertical axis and the units of production along the horizontal. The amount of the sales can, if it is wished, be substituted for units on the horizontal.

The fixed cost line is first plotted and it will normally be found to be parallel to the horizontal axis showing how, over the range of production, the level does not vary.

Next the total cost line will be plotted. The amount is found by adding the variable costs to the fixed costs for several volumes and joining the line. The starting point will be where the fixed cost line cuts the vertical axis.

Lastly, the sales line is put in. It is calculated for a given volume of sales (volume × unit price) and a line drawn from the axis intersection.

Where the sales line cuts the total cost line, this is the break-even point. Activity above this point is profitable but below will be loss making.

By extending a line from a chosen volume of production up to the sales line it is possible to measure the amount of profit which may be earned. The measurement will be the distance between the total cost and the sales lines at the point.

Another use of such a chart is to measure the margin of safety. Forecasts do not always materialize as it is hoped and it is useful to be aware of how far production can drop without a loss-making situation occurring. This is found by measuring the distance from the break even to the desired level. By converting the units of production to money terms, the possible drop in revenue can be seen and this figure can be used in formulating a pricing policy. These features can be seen in fig. 15.

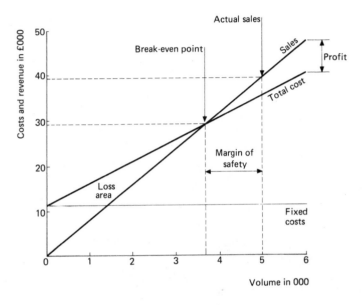

Fig. 15 Break-even chart.

Sometimes to illustrate the marginal effect the fixed costs are imposed upon the variables to give the total cost line. This is shown in fig.16.

Above the break-even point the readings are as before but it does permit the contribution to be measured should, for any reason, the production be forced to drop drastically. By reading the chart the management can see the result of the decisions they must make.

For example, if due to a power failure for a long period, production could reach only one-quarter of the planned level, the contribution to the fixed costs could be seen and a decision made whether it was worth continuing to produce at the low level or whether it would be better to close down completely.

In this case the area between the variable cost line and the sales line represents the marginal income.

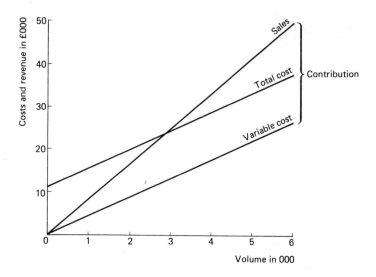

Fig. 16   Break-even chart showing marginal income.

Other charts show how the information can be supplemented with a breakdown of the fixed and variable costs; the use of a chart to show the effect of an increase in the sales price; the increase in total fixed costs; and finally the effect of an increase in the variable costs (fig.17).

There is a limit to the application of the charts other than that produced by their inherent degree of inaccuracy. In the cases examined it has been assumed the factors change in isolation. In practice this is not so. An increase in the fixed cost can bring about a drop in the variable costs. This could be by the production unit becoming more capital intensive. Another example could arise when there is a reduction in the price. Then

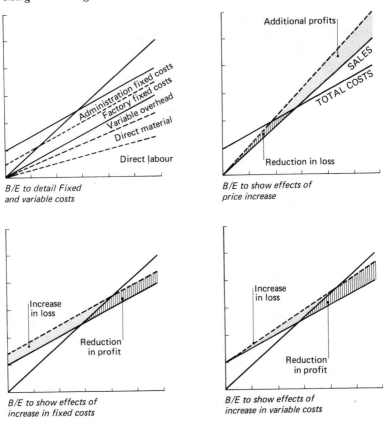

Fig. 17   Variations on break-even charts.

there is an increase in the number sold and by being able to operate with greater efficiency the variable costs fall.

The other limitation can arise when more than one product is being considered. The charts used have given the impression that the business has only one product or only one product is being considered at a time. Again, in practice, this is rarely the situation and a variation in the sales mix – the proportion of the various products in the total sales – can have repercussions on both the variable and the fixed costs.

However, even with these limitations, the use of the break-even chart is widespread and is a useful aid in the planning process.

Profit/Volume

With the interplay the elements of cost and sales have with the profits, the standard break-even calculation is not sufficient when planning. It may be necessary to simulate the effects of a sales campaign or of a drop in price for the period of a sales promotion.

In connection with this, in the multi-product business, it is essential to know which product is profitable and which is not and also to see how any change of emphasis will effect each part.

It is useful to know, as well, the effect on the breakdown under the changing conditions.

The study of this aspect is by the examination of the profit related to the volume of production and the interplay between them. It can be carried out by calculations made in columnar form but this is inclined to become a mass of figures and not very easy to interpret.

It is better, as in the calculation with the break even, to present the information in graphical form.

This is shown in fig.18. The graph is divided horizontally by the sales line expressed in money. The area above the line is reserved for profit and the area below for costs (or losses).

Construction is simple. The amount of the fixed cost is marked off on the left hand margin (below the sales line as it is a cost) and the computed profit is marked off above the sales line on the right hand margin.

This profit is computed on the sales for the 'end of the line'. The length of the sales line represents the expected level of sales of all products.

The break-even point for the business is where the line drawn to join the fixed cost point on the left hand margin to the profit point on the right, cuts across the sales line.

The effects of altering the level of the fixed costs or the profit can be dealt with very easily.

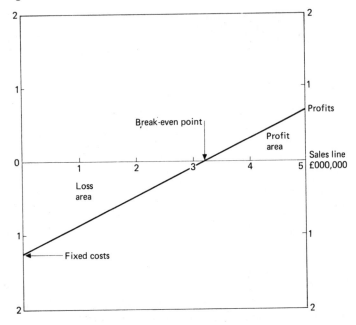

Fig. 18   Profit/volume chart.

This overcomes the objection to the break-even chart – that its various elements may have sympathic movement. Here the sales revenue can be made up for several products without effect. If the variable costs vary, these are reflected in the total profit and should a change in the product mix alter the level of the fixed costs, this can be adjusted without trouble.

In fig. 19, the concept is taken further with an analysis of the product contribution. One of the features needed is a knowledge of the extent of the contribution the particular product is making to the whole of the profit. This is not to say that, if it is seen that a product is not fulfilling its expected quota, it should be eliminated.

A study should be made and, provided there is a contribution, it should be left in the product range. On the other hand, if by maintaining production in that area resources are being diverted from another product which contributes more and can

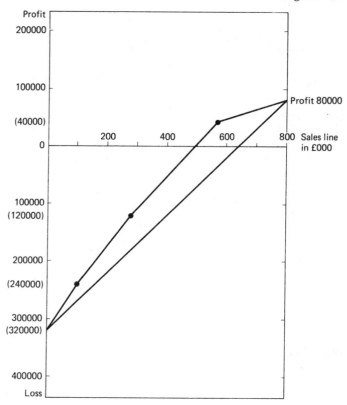

Fig. 19   Profit/volume chart to show analysis of contribution.

be sold to make good a sales deficiency, then a change in the mix is called for. The P/V analysis graph will show this.

The graph is constructed as before with the line connecting fixed costs and profit but in addition a line is constructed to show each contribution, product by product.

First taken is the product with the highest P/V ratio, or, as it is sometimes known, the MARGINAL INCOME RATIO.

Marginal income is the excess of sales revenue over the variable costs and can be found for any given volume of production. If it is accepted in a product that the variable costs are

111

constant for each unit of production, then with the selling price at a given level, the marginal income must also be constant (as well as being fixed for a given volume).

It is the contribution available in each unit of production and if this expressed against the unit of sales as a percentage (for example against per £ of sales) the result is the Profit/Volume Ratio or more normally the P/V ratio.

To revert to plotting the graph, using the product with the highest P/V ratio, and assuming the product has a sales level of £100,000 and a P/V ratio of 80%, the contribution is £80,000. For convenience this will be called product A.

The total cost graph shows the fixed costs for producing products A to D is £320,000, so if £80,000 is recovered through A, there remains £240,000 to collect.

This is represented by drawing a line from the fixed cost point at £320,000 to £240,000 in the lower loss area directly below the sales for product A (£100,000).

Product B has sales of £180,000 and a P/V ratio of $66\frac{2}{3}$% with a money contribution of £120,000.

The profit line for B starts where A ceases and runs to the loss area level of £120,000 (there has now been a recovery of £200,000 − £80,000 for A and £120,000 for B). This will be below the point of the total combined sales for products A and B, £280,000.

Repeat the process for product C which has sales of £280,000 and a P/V ratio of 57% and this will take the profit line into the upper profit area.

Finally take product D, with the lowest ratio of $16\frac{2}{3}$% on sales of £240,000.

This will bring the profit line back to the original total profit point of £80,000 on sales of £800,000.

The contribution effort by each product can be seen by the steepness of the line and should a line go downwards, not upwards, this means that the product concerned is not only failing to make a profit but is failing to contribute any marginal income.

In the example given, the shallowness of the slope for product D makes it doubtful whether it is profitable and a calculation would be needed for this.

In fact with the P/V of 16⅔%, the variable costs would be £200,000 which when taken on a total variable cost would be 50% of that figure. On the same basis the proportion of fixed costs to be attributed to product D should be 50% or £160,000. This gives a total cost for D as £360,000 making a loss of £120,000 on a sales value of £240,000 or a 50% loss on sales.

The immediate reaction with a loss of that apparent magnitude would be to discontinue production immediately but as was mentioned earlier the product is contributing to the overall profit by covering some of the fixed charges. Unless there is another product which can take up the capacity (and be sold) as well as make a greater contribution, it is better to have some contribution than no contribution at all.

Marginal Costing in Pricing

Many times when selling, the opportunity comes to produce against a special order which can be dealt with within the capacity of the factory. Often the decision has to be made whether to accept or not as the price permitted seems so low that only a loss can be made. This very often happens when dealing in the export market.

To assist in making the decision, the use of marginal costing is essential and the following example may make the situation clear.

XYZ Co. Ltd manufactures bodgers, highly regarded in industry for the temporary repair of machinery. At present the output is 100,000 units, all of which are sold on the domestic market at £10 each. The variable cost is £5 per unit and for this production the fixed costs are at £2 per unit leaving £3 as profit. The factory is working at only two-thirds capacity.

In totals this means the factory has the following results:

Sales		£1,000,000
less variable costs	£500,000	
fixed costs	200,000	
		700,000
Profit		£ 300,000

113

The directors were most anxious to obtain more sales to make full use of the facilities available.

One day the sales manager received in the post an order from an overseas customer for 50,000 bodgers but unless they could be supplied at a price of £6.75 each, the order would go to a supplier in another country which could supply at £6.70 with a slightly lower quality.

The production manager was overjoyed for here was the chance to reach maximum capacity but some of the directors believed the whole order, useful as it would be, must be rejected. They felt it would be wrong to sell at a loss, merely to keep the capacity of the factory up to a maximum. After all, from the costing system it was shown the total cost per unit was £7 and if the selling price was £6.75 there would be a loss on the order of £12,500.

Of course, the accounting staff, from their knowledge of the marginal costing principles, knew this would not be so, but they had to convince the directors.

They presented to them a statement to show the expected final result for the year if the order were taken:

Sales	(£1,000,000 + £337,500)	£1,337,500
less costs:		
variable	£750,000	
fixed	200,000	
		950,000
Profit		£ 387,500

The directors were delighted but were still somewhat sceptical and wanted an explanation.

The answer lies in the fixed costs. While the variable costs amount to £5 per unit no matter where the bodgers go, the fixed costs remain static in total so that instead of their being charged out at £2 per unit, they can now be spread over a greater number of 150,000 giving an average of £1.33 per unit. The higher capacity used will result in the unit costs falling.

If put in marginal terms, in both cases the variable costs will remain at £5 per unit but there is a contribution from each towards the recovery of the fixed costs of £5 from the domestic sales and £1.75 per unit from the export order. In total this contribution came to £500,000 from the domestic and £87,500 from the special – in all £587,500 – but as the fixed costs were only £200,000, the remainder was a profit of £387,500.

This shows that if there is a contribution from a product, however small it may be, there will always be an improvement in the overall profit position.

Chapter Twelve

Standard Costing

Most systems of costing use either actual costs or standard costs. The system mentioned so far has been dealing with actual costs which must by their nature depend upon historical events.

An alternative is to use a standard cost applied through a standard costing system. As the name implies there are two parts, the standard and the cost. Costs have already been described although in this application they are at a predetermined rate.

The standard implies method and measurement. In fact the whole system depends upon predetermined costs set up as they *should* be incurred by measurement and study of the method of operation.

In practice this is a system similar to marginal costing in as much as it allows a closer study of cost behaviour than historical costing but although it can be used right through the whole of the operation of the business, it is usually confined to a restricted area.

In the manufacturing operations of a business full benefit can be derived but in the selling and administration it is much harder to apply.

There is no reason why standard costing should not be applied to the manufacturing function leaving a budgetary control system (as will be discussed in the next chapter) for the other functions.

The main benefit is that the costs never vary and this means there should be quicker reporting available. Any deviations (known as variances) from the standards can be seen if the actual results are compared and by applying the principle of management by exception, time is not wasted in finding where the organization is straying from its planned path.

Another benefit which comes from the use of a standard costing system is almost a by-product. To make sure the standards are set correctly there has to be investigation both into use of material and labour necessary to convert it and into the methods which are used. This type of investigation usually reveals weaknesses, waste and ineffective working. Once these are corrected the organization should be able to operate with greater efficiency and, in turn, should be able to recover the cost of the investigation in the first place.

Standards

The whole system is dependent on the correct setting of the standards. As far as is possible they should be correct the first time, for although they can be changed if the defect is large, a number of changes occurring rapidly may be misleading when trying to interpret the results. Many changes also have a detrimental effect on the labour force who normally gauge their own performance on the standards set for them, and where their wages are linked through a bonus or other incentive scheme, changes become a very important matter.

Two main types of standard are set, the BASIC STANDARD and the CURRENT STANDARD.

The basic standard is the yardstick against which future performances may be measured. If an economic index is compared with this, the basic is the index number, usually 100, against which the later performance is measured. Changes in the basic standards are rare and should occur only when important changes are made in the components or the manufacturing method.

Current standards are the standards set for a limited period and applied to a given expected set of circumstances and conditions. Revisions are made to reflect changes in prices and method.

In an integrated system of accounting, standards can be introduced into the financial books in place of actual costs with variations between the actual and the standard treated as a measurement of efficiency.

Most companies use the current standards rather than the basic standard.

Within each type of standard there are three 'sub-types' which can be chosen to suit the needs and preference of the management.

Firstly there can be the 'ideal' standard which is set to reflect the theoretical or maximum level of efficiency. It is rare for this standard to be reached and even more rare for the attainment to be sustained. As a guide to management they are not particularly useful and from the viewpoint of the worker they have an adverse psychological effect as to attain success is beyond the competence of most of them.

At the other extreme, standards can be set to reflect the expected levels in the next year and to take into consideration conditions caused by mistakes, by wastages and operating. All these things are likely to happen but this really does defeat the purpose of the system which is to show what *should* occur and not what is expected.

Most companies compromise and set the standards at what should happen under normal circumstances. It may be an average figure but it will be set at a level of reasonable efficiency. It will not be too low or else there will be no incentive; it will be, for labour, at a level which the competent worker can just reach but does not exceed all the time.

The System

Once the standards are fixed the whole of the costs for the operations can be planned by taking the number of units it is intended to produce and multiplying these by the standard costs.

Overheads take a secondary role and are introduced through a rate based on the direct costs.

This shows that there are two important factors to be brought into standard costing and both will be examined. There is the criterion on which the system is based, and the target for the company to reach. The first is in the standards and the second by the corrections to course highlighted by the examination of the variances.

This very important part comes by a subsequent study of the actual to find why the target was not reached or sometimes, just as bad, why it was exceeded.

Setting Standards

Although standard costing is a financial system, both the physical and the financial aspects need to be taken into consideration when setting the standards.

Once set, they need to be stable for an agreed period of time. In some organizations this may be a period of six months, in others a year. The most important thing is for the standard to remain for as long a time as is possible and this implies that the setting will be methodical and thorough. Too many alterations cause the workforce to lose faith in the standard, especially if the change is due to internal influences rather than being brought about by external factors not under the control of the standard setters.

Most of the standards are based on the past performance for, although the system is essentially forward looking, things that have happened before play an important role. To obtain the best from these, there needs to be an intensive study of past events, unless a new business is being studied.

If it is a new product in an existing business that is contemplated, some of the study procedure will be to construct the new from the parts of the old and then to check upon the result from other sources and methods.

The starting point, in manufacturing, will be the product design specification. From this both the material and labour costs can be built up – the material by simple reference to prices and the labour from a study of the design to find the time needed to complete the component and to estimate the skill and level of worker required.

A by-product which often emerges from the study of the design to relate it to the manufacturing process, is the finding of a more efficient method. As a study in depth is made of all the movements and processes necessary, quicker and improved ways are found which more than cover the cost, through their savings, of the motion and method study.

Material standards

Two aspects arise from material costs and for each a separate standard needs to be developed. These are the PRICE STANDARD and the USAGE STANDARD.

The price standard represents the market price and there can be very little control exercised over this by the management. They may be able to obtain a price reduction on the quoted price due to the size of the order or the strength of the purchasing company but other than substituting one material for another, the management is dependent on the market price.

Price standards are usually fixed for one year ahead and should reflect possible and probable price changes. It may mean the standard is above the actual at the beginning of the year but in the analysis of the variance this will be obvious. When there are large and sudden increases in price, which are likely to be permanent, it is the usual practice to change the standard during the year, although to control this change through variance analysis would not be wrong.

Whether a change is made depends upon the price pattern of the material. If the price is subject to violent fluctuations changes would not be made. Management policy will play a role in this as well.

To find the standard materials cost for the product or the component, the standard quantity as discovered from the specification is multiplied by the standard price.

The control exercised is by studying the reasons why the actual price differs. If the actual materials cost is above the standard cost there is said to be an adverse variance, if better than standard, in this case below, it is a favourable variance.

Note how the variance is expressed in relation to the standard and that, by itself, a favourable variance is not always good for the business as, due to the inter-relationship of costs, there could be an adverse variance elsewhere which more than compensates.

Material usage standard

As well as knowing how much the material should cost it is necessary to know if the quantity being used is correct. It may be that the actual quantity is in excess and there are a variety of reasons which can be found on analysis.

The quality can be poor so there is a higher level of wastage, the methods may be wrong so the spoilt work is high or possibly it is necessary to use operators with a lower level of skills than planned and so more material is used.

All this information is based on the physical aspects and only comes to light when the standard material cost is broken down into its two prime components of price and usage.

To establish the usage needs co-operation between the engineering and the accounting staff. In a large organization the product engineering department will need to be involved for they can calculate how much material goes into the making of a part. They will start with the standard material specifications and for a new product will build on the experience gained from other products.

Once the standard quantity in the product has been fixed, the amounts to be used will be revised upwards to allow for the extra material which will be consumed through wastage, seepage, evaporation or whatever the nature of the material warrants as well as for some spoilage.

After one year it is likely the quantity standard will have to be revised as it takes time to establish the percentage of wastage, spoilage, etc. which comes into every process.

Having to revise after one year and possibly again after the following year, is not a sign of weakness. It is unusual for the figures to be exactly right the first time, it takes years to get a smooth system working but the benefits are there from the very beginning. Examining the variances to find why there is a difference shows up any inefficiencies and leads the organization back to its chosen course.

Variances

Material variances

With the standards fixed and agreed, production starts and soon after the end of the first control period the reports appear. They show both the standard material cost and the actual material cost for the period. For subsequent periods it is likely that not only will the figures be for the single month but there will also be the accumulated totals for the year to date. The standard and actual are always compared, not actual and last year as these bear no relationship to each other.

The material quantity variance is calculated by taking the actual quantity priced at standard price with the standard quantity priced at standard price.

Using some basic information:
Standard Price per tonne	£10
Standard quantity per unit of product	200 tonnes
Actual price per tonne	£10
Actual usage per unit	195 tonnes

The calculation will be:

Actual cost per unit (195 × £10)	£1,950
Standard cost per unit (200 × £10)	2,000
Variance (favourable)	£ 50

As the actual cost is below the standard cost the result is better than expected and the variance is favourable.

Shown graphically it would appear as in fig. 20.

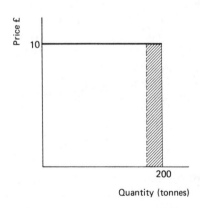

Fig. 20   Favourable material variance.

With the actual quantity falling within the line formed by the standard it must be a favourable variance.

On the other hand if instead of the actual usage being 195 tonnes, it was 205 tonnes, the variance would be:

Actual cost per unit	£2,050
Standard cost per unit	2,000
Variance (adverse)	£ 50

As the actual cost is above the standard cost the variance is adverse. On the graphical presentation (fig. 21) it shows outside the standard line.

If the graph is to scale, the amount can be calculated by measurement.

If there is a price variance, which is caused by the actual price of the material being higher or lower than the standard, the calculation is made by taking the actual cost per standard unit and comparing it with the standard cost for the standard unit.

Using the basic detail from the previous example, excepting that the actual price per tonne is firstly £8 and then £11.

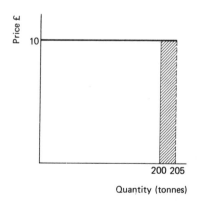

Fig. 21   Adverse material variance.

At £8 per tonne the variance is:

Actual cost per unit (200 × £8)	£1,600
Standard cost per unit (200 × £10)	2,000
Favourable variance	£ 400

or at £11 per tonne:

Actual cost per unit (200 × £11)	£2,200
Standard cost per unit	2,000
Adverse price variance	£ 200

Sometimes the price and usage variances are combined. In this case the actual price is multiplied by the actual usage, to be compared with the standard quantity multiplied by the standard price. To take a simple example where both variances are favourable and the data:

Standards as before	
Actual price per tonne	£8
Actual usage per unit	195 tonne

The variance is calculated as:

Actual cost per unit (195 × £8)	£1,560
Standard cost per unit (200 × £10)	2,000
Favourable variance	£ 440

It may seem strange that this figure is not the sum of the two separate variances but this is caused by an overlap which is demonstrated by the graphical picture (fig. 22). The common area is added to one or the other but not to both. Sometimes this 'area' is treated as a separate variance but this is beyond the scope of this book.

Labour variances
As in the materials variances there are variances of both price and usage for labour although they are given different names. The price variance comes from the price of labour – the wage rates paid for the job to be done – and the usage is the time

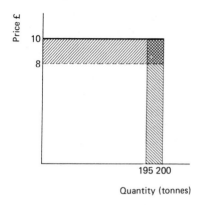

Fig. 22   Price and usage variance combined.

taken to do the job. Both are, of course, compared with the standard.

Calculation for the wage rate variance is:

Actual cost per unit (actual wage rate × standard time allowed) less the standard cost per unit (standard wage rate × standard time allowed).

Favourable and adverse variances follow the usual rules.

Variances are caused by having to use labour at a higher or lower rate than was planned or having to pay at a higher rate due to a wages award negotiated through a trade union or similar body.

The labour efficiency ratio takes the standard wage rate and the actual time taken and compares it with the standard cost per unit.

Combined variances can be found by comparing the actual cost per unit (actual wages × actual time) with the standard labour cost per unit.

Differences which arise can be for a variety of reasons such as the use of unsuitable machinery causing a drop in the production rate, industrial troubles such as a go-slow, a breakdown in the factory production or merely the use of unsuitable labour.

Overhead variances

In standard costing there is a charge made to the production for the overhead and is based, for the variable portion of the overhead, on the machine hour rate. For the fixed overhead, a similar rate is established but cannot be linked so closely to the level of production. Obviously variances arise and, to calculate for the overhead spending variance, compare the actual overhead with the overhead applied to the production. The standard in this case is the budgeted machine hour rate and this can be taken as a basis for the examination of efficiency.

Efficiency variances are based on the labour rate and the actual hours taken, multiplied by standard rate and the result is compared with the standard (or budgeted hours) multiplied by standard rate.

Volume variances are brought in to control the application of the fixed overhead which is governed by the level of production to the extent that the greater the production, the less must be the amount per unit produced.

Variances are also calculated for yields and mix. The first looks at the result of obtaining a yield from production which differs from the one planned on the basis of the input. The mix variance examines the result of mixing the basic raw materials in different quantities from the planned standard.

These are only a few of the variances used in standard costing and the reader needing more information is directed to one of the standard texts. Many are sophisticated and a great deal of information about the performance of the business can be obtained as they are analysed.

However, it needs to be stressed most strongly that the calculation of the variances and their analysis with explanations of their meaning are worthless to managers, unless there is subsequent action. The variance shows that the results are not as planned and action is needed to rectify or in some other way balance the revealed situation.

Chapter Thirteen

Forecasts, Budgets and Budgetary Control

In business there is just as much a need as in private life, to plan and to look ahead to the future. It can be done just by sitting back in a chair and dreaming of things to come or it can be put onto a more formal basis by writing down the ideas, arranging them into a sensible order and, after considering the plan to be feasible, trying to stick to it.

When these future plans are made by a business, the terms FORECASTING and BUDGETING are used.

A forecast is a prediction of what is likely to happen in the future in a given set of circumstances and as with all predictions into the future, needs judgement, or more bluntly, guesses. Provided the guess is based on reasonable assumptions there is nothing wrong but it must be realized that the further the guess or forecast goes into the future the less accurate it can be.

In spite of that limitation, a forecast can be of great use. At least, it means that some thought has been given to the future and a target set for what is hoped to be attained.

In a business a forecast can be made to show the anticipated state of the company in ten years' time with forecasts for two, three or five years ahead as well. The time that can be predicted must depend on the nature of the business.

A forecast cannot be too detailed due to the time scale but for a business to be guided along a path for success it needs to see the immediate future, so the day to day decisions can be made which will bring the plan into action.

This is done by a budget, a plan in financial terms. It differs from the forecast as it is not a judgement but a cost plan related to a period of time. It is planned scheme to attain the objectives of the business and once it has been approved by the management it becomes the executive order to put the plan into action.

General Aims and Objectives

Planning involves calculation of the profits necessary to pay the investors but far more important, there is the human aspect, the co-ordinating and control of people who will make the profits a reality.

This does not mean that if the need for profit is not present, nothing should be done. In some organizations where profit is not the objective, the planning is to make sure there is a break-even with the costs equalling the revenue.

The techniques are just as important in organizations which raise their funds from grants, gifts or donations. Here the objective is to put the income available to the best possible use and this can be done only through planned expenditure.

Whichever need relates to a particular business or organization, the planning, whether forecasting or budgeting, must retain the human involvement and be a guide to human behaviour. At some point a person must press the button to start the whole process.

Advantages

These are many but one of the foremost is the need to start by studying the problem to see what can be done and then to lay down a policy to be followed to overcome the problem.

As time moves ahead, there is a need to revise the forecasts and budgets and each time this occurs, there is a necessity to review the problems, to re-examine them and maybe to devise a new policy. As the re-appraisal is made, weaknesses are shown up and, through this, wastage of manpower and resources can be avoided.

In the business field these financial plans direct the capital and the effort of the organization towards the most profitable areas, and in doing so allow the management to see where it has to raise the long-term and short-term finance.

Limitations

A fact which is often overlooked is that forecasting and budgeting need a degree of judgement, forecasting needing more than budgeting. Neither can be exact as they are looking to what the future is expected to be.

There is a myth of accuracy and rigidity which is often introduced into budgets. Because the budget is agreed at a certain level, managers are afraid to exceed it for fear of the consequences. At no time should a budget be used as a weapon to beat a subordinate. It is a guide towards achieving the planned target and the idea of examining the variances from the plan, is to determine what changes must be made.

Of course, the examination may show up some gross mis-management, but that is a different matter.

Normally, where there is a difference, the actual percentage must depend on policy or the type of expense and the manager has to explain the reason. It may be that a lucrative order was placed or, due to industrial unrest, some deliveries had to be made in an unplanned manner at greater cost.

What must not happen is for the budget to be treated as a strait-jacket. For example, if there was an order ready to be placed in India, it would be defeating the purpose of planning if the representative could not be sent out because there was nothing left in the sales promotion budget. Or, in another case, as the labour budget had been exceeded overtime could not be worked on an export order carrying a penalty clause.

One effect of a rigid policy is to tempt the supervisor or manager to adjust the actual figures to make sure they do come out right or within the levels of tolerance and so avoid trouble for himself. Then, any budgetary scheme becomes worthless.

No budgetary scheme can replace management. It is only an aid to help them to make the decisions necessary to achieve the profit goals.

In doing this, one point is often overlooked. For a budgetary system to be successful, it must be thought out properly and that needs time. If the scheme is drafted at the last moment, points of importance will be missed. Time must be allowed to set the budgets, to make sure they are complimentary and finally to ensure that they are communicated to those who are to carry them out.

The only area in which speed is essential is in reporting the actual and this becomes of less use as time goes by.

Needs of Budgeting

For a budgetary system to be successful, it needs clear thinking at the planning stage mixed with commonsense. The expectations which are produced as a budget must be realistic. It is not of any use to incorporate into a sales budget, a target, which could be met only by the market leader while the company concerned commands only 5% of the market. To allow that to happen will mean that the staff will merely laugh at the targets they are supposed to attain and then ignore them.

This will often occur when the targets are imposed 'from above'. The top management will set the targets without reference to those below or will add to the expected performance.

One company selling stationery made it their official policy to raise the budgeted target of their sales force by 10% every year. Not only did the staff fail to reach the targets but very soon they found more amenable employment with other companies.

From this it can be seen there must be total commitment to the system, not only by the employees who have to make the planned profit a reality but also from the management at all levels to the very top.

Top management must not just pay lip service, they must make sure that the system is being operated correctly, that the budgets are realistic and, most important of all, that action is taken on deviations from the plan.

Another need is for the budgetary system to be linked with responsibility accounting. If budgets are to be set by the staff who are going to carry out the work, it is right that they should bear the responsibility for their ideas being carried out.

Of course, their first plan might not be accepted but it will be adjusted to blend in with the plans and aspirations of colleagues and balanced by the capabilities of the organization as a whole. Once it is agreed at the cost or profit centre concerned, it is carried out or any differences arising must be explained.

The last need for a system is for the persons setting the budgets to remember that they are not playing with numbers or money. Budgets are the planned outcome of physical resources of a business, the labour, the machines, the raw material and so on, translated into money terms as a common standard of measurement. If the physical aspect were kept in mind more often, many more budgets would be realistic.

Principal Budget Factor

It appears to be very easy to study the organization, the market, the economic situation and then to combine them all together to produce the master budget. Unfortunately this is only a dream.

In each organization lurks some factor which will prevent the plan from being put into action freely. There is always a restraining factor which stops management doing as it would like. It may be a lack of capital, insufficient capacity, no suitable labour or a depression in the market.

One factor of this nature will always be more dominant than the others and the most disturbing fact of life is that once this has been cured another will take its place.

In practical terms, it means all planning must be made to take these factors into consideration and the budgets adjusted to accommodate them.

Organizing for Budgets

In the large organization there can be a separate management team whose task it is to draw up the budgets and to monitor the performance.

In the smaller business the task falls in the first place on the accountant who will then structure the budgets together with the senior managers and finally get approval by the managing director.

If size permits, a budgetary committee will be appointed from the senior management and with them will be a budget officer. His role will be to act as the committee secretary and to pass on the instructions from the committee. His task does not stop there, for he will have to make sure the timetable is adhered to throughout the company when drawing up the budgets and, when they do arrive in, he will have to co-ordinate them to make sure they are compatible. It would be useless for the sales department to submit a sales target of one million

131

units of a product when the factory at full capacity can produce only half a million.

His skill will be used to draw up the budget programme in the first place and he will advise the committee. Before he can draw up the programme he will have had to study the organization in depth.

This is one of the extra advantages of a budget system. For a plan and policy to be made, the company structure must be known together with details of all the various jobs, who is reporting to whom and the responsibility of each manager.

All of this will be found in the budget manual which is circulated and in this is the organization chart. By showing the organization in chart form as well as by description, the inter-relationships can be seen. Charts will also show the work-flow and one of the additional tasks falling to the budget officer will be to make sure these are all up to date.

It is very easy for changes to be made without their being recorded in the manual. All will be well until the next budget is drawn up on the wrong information and the differences which are soon shown up could destroy the base of the whole budget.

Putting Budgeting into Action

One of the first tasks will be to decide the budget periods. The main period will have to be based on one planning cycle although in practice the natural cycle of one year is usually adopted. To add to the convenience, the year usually coincides with the financial year of the company.

A period of a year is too long for control purposes and a great deal can happen in this time, not only from factors external to the business, but also internally as well. There is a need to break the year down and this is done into monthly or four-weekly periods.

Monthly periods have the advantage of being used with the normal calendar and most people know when the month starts and ends. On the other hand, the length of each month differs, making comparison from one month to another difficult.

To combat this, the four-week period was introduced. All periods are equal, so comparison can be made with ease but there are disadvantages. In a year there are not quite thirteen sub-periods, so every few years an extra week has to be added to bring it back into line with the calendar.

The calendar is also the cause of the other disadvantage. As the year progresses it becomes increasingly difficult to know when the next period begins and unless a separate calendar is issued or the four-week periods super-imposed on normal year calendars, chaos will result.

Variations in the periods to attempt to solve the length of periods are many, and one is to use two four-week periods followed by a five-week period in each quarter.

One advantage will be found from using the sub-control periods and that is the ability to introduce seasonal factors or production variations into the budgets.

Not all the budgets can be put conveniently into short control periods as the nature of the item opposes this. For example the capital budget spans several years and to try to control the spending in this budget to a particular control period would not show any great advantages. The expenditure control for this area will be in the cash budget.

A budget for research and development will come under the same category but the control span is not as long. 'R and D' covers a year or more but it is usually impossible to tell just when the research will produce the required result.

The cash budget was mentioned above. This looks at the proposed inflow and outflow of cash, whether it is in respect of operating expenditure of for capital purposes. As cash is vital to the continued existence of the company, this budget is some-times taken beyond the normal sub-periods to a daily basis. The method of dealing with cash will be referred to later.

Constructing the Budget

There are two main methods of constructing the budget. Either it can be imposed on the workforce from above or the managers responsible for the various cost centres can take part by suggest-ing the budgets for their own sector and, then, having the whole brought together to make sure it is compatible throughout the organization.

Arguments can be put forward for each. With the imposed budget, it can be said that only the top management can see the overall picture and the outside influences and so are the only ones placed to take a balanced view. In practice when this is done, it is the sales budget and the production budget which are fixed in this way and at the next stage in the management structure the related budgets are added.

An imposed budget does have the great disadvantage that unless the management are in very close touch with the whole organization they may be setting targets which are unrealistic and which will tend to be ignored or even ridiculed.

If the opposite course is taken with the budget being set initially at the lowest level possible and gradually built up to a whole, the responsibility for non-compliance falls back on the person who constructed his own targets. There are disadvantages. People are inclined to think only of their own sphere of activity and not of the organization as a whole, and so each individual budget needs to be taken and blended with the rest. As the blending takes place, and as managers vet them to see if they are realistic, some parts may be reduced and others increased.

This is perfectly in order provided that before any cuts or upward revisions are made the maker of the budget is informed and is able to put his viewpoint on the change. If this is not done the manager at the setting level will tend in the future to treat the process as a futile exercise and will feel it does not really matter what he says.

Another bad practice may arise from cuts in the proposed expenditure without some consultation. There is the time-honoured procedure of deciding what is needed, then doubling the figure, as it is known that when top management receive the budget they will have to be seen to make cuts and halve the proposal. This practice normally leads to a waste of money by the budget controller who, finding at the end of the year he has underspent, places orders for the balance in the fear that, if he does not, it will be presumed that his previous allotment was too high and therefore his new budget must be reduced.

All these discussions on the new budgets to be fixed take time. It would be useless for them to be issued after the start of the period covered, remembering that once approved they become the executive order for the year. If the budget period was to start on 1 January, it would be necessary for the approved budget to be communicated to all by the middle of the preceding December with the primary discussions needing to be started at about the beginning of September.

This gives time for all the initial budget proposals to be received and brought together, the necessary revisions to be made for compatibility and the approval procedure to be followed by the top management.

Top management needs to be consulted for, unless they give their whole-hearted commitment to budgeting, then there is a reduced possibility of co-operation at lower levels.

At first the policy of the company will have to be reviewed and from this any changes to the forecasts introduced. Then, within this framework, the budgeting can begin, usually on a functional basis.

As the modern tendency is to produce what can be sold rather than to sell the production of a factory at full capacity, the sales budget comes first. To this is related the main production budget.

Once these are reconciled, the subsidiary budgets are built up. For example, for the sales, there would be budgets for the costs of the sales force, for sales promotion and for distribution. Production would produce budgets for purchasing, for stores costs, labour and many others while the administration would be likely to produce their budgets on a departmental basis to reflect their needs for the forthcoming period.

After considerable 'juggling' the operating budgets would be completed and ready to be blended with the capital budget into the master budget.

While this is proceeding, the budget for the capital needs would be looked at. This would be for the purchase of new or replacement equipment. Once this and the operating budgets are complete the cash requirement can be planned.

At this stage other budgets can be brought in. All the expenditure needs to be financed. The capital budget may need extra funds brought in from outside the company, as may the working capital budget.

It is just as important to control and manage the working capital overall, as it is any one section, such as the cash. This budget is a co-ordinating budget, taking its main elements from other sections. Stock budgets will have been dealt with in various parts of the production budget whether as raw materials or finished goods. Debtors and creditors will need to be calculated for the cash flow but will need a detailed study in their own right.

Once all these budgets are completed they are brought together to form a budgeted profit and loss account and by the incorporation of the capital and working capital budgets with the past situation, a budgeted balance sheet can be produced. This will show the expected financial position at the end of the period. It is the detailed year made up from the forecasts which stretches away into the future, again, usually presented in balance sheet form.

The budgeted balance sheet often goes under the name of the MASTER BUDGET.

Flexible Budgets

One limitation of normal budgeting is that it allows no recognition of any change in the level of the expense should the production or the sales fail to reach or exceed the budgeted figure. In many businesses this fluctuation can be of great significance.

To combat this defect a system of flexible budgeting has been introduced. It attempts to relate overheads to the volume of production.

The starting point is the chosen volume for the main budget and the overheads calculated around this. One of three levels of production can be chosen – the theoretical capacity, the practical capacity or the normal capacity.

With the chosen capacity taken as 100%, the overheads for this level are worked out and then re-calculated for levels above and below. This would be based on experience of how the planned volume is likely to vary. For example, below could be at 95, 90 and 85% with the above rate at 105 and 110%.

It is not possible to take the expenses in the overhead and to adjust them in a similar manner. This is due to those expenses which remain fixed and those which have a degree of movement dependent on the volume. An example of a flexible budget is given in fig. 23.

Budget and Capacity	% 80	% 90	% 100	% 110	% 120
	£	£	£	£	£
Variable Overhead	1,530	1,650	1,800	2,040	2,310
Fixed Overhead	1,200	1,200	1,200	1,200	1,200
Total Overhead	2,730	2,850	3,000	3,240	3,510

Note: The budget would be shown in greater detail and possibly related through direct wages to a labour charge. By extrapolation intermediate rates are found.

Direct Wages (hours)	800	900	1,000	1,100	1,200
Overhead Rate per hour (overhead÷hours)	£3.41	£3.17	£3	£2.95	£2.93

Fig. 23   XYZ Ltd., budget for Dept. 7, for 19——.

If flexible budgeting can be used, a much more realistic view can be taken of the events when they occur and the control is made easier.

Budgetary Control

As has been mentioned many times, it is useless to produce a mass of information on a business and then to file it away, never to expose it to the light of day again. It may as well not be produced in the first place.

It is the same with budgeting. Making the plan is one thing, putting it into action is another but the task and responsibility do not stop there. Some form of monitoring must be introduced to make sure the plan is being followed. If it is not, then the appropriate action must be taken to correct the course.

To supply the monitoring information, budgetary control has been developed very successfully.

As soon as possible after the end of each control period, information is produced under the same headings as in the budgets, and reports are prepared for the management at various levels with the actual results compared with the budget predictions. If there are any differences, investigations are made, reasons given and any necessary corrective action taken.

It is a waste of time examining differences when they come within a pre-agreed tolerance, as to go deeply into 1% difference could be to no avail. The budget was a forecast based on construction of a future event and the chances of being exactly right are remote.

In practice, if the actual does come out exactly in line with the budget, it probably does need to be examined more closely. The chances are, out of misguided loyalty, there has been a re-allocation of results to make sure it looks as planned. Sometimes this attitude is created by the top management who do not really understand the true concept of budgeting and use it as a weapon to bludgeon their subordinates if there is a difference. They fail to see that there should be some difference and their attention should be re-directed to where this is important.

The level of the difference needing investigation depends on the nature of the business concerned and the policy and needs of the management.

This is another example of 'management by exception'. Time is not wasted on the matters which are going correctly but the effort is put to where things are wrong.

As was said above, the actual results are prepared for all levels of management. In the same way as the budgets were made at each cost or profit centre and the responsibility laid with the manager controlling the centre, so are the results given.

In this way corrections can be made as the manager concerned can see quickly if it is his actions that are the cause. It could be that there is a difference caused by another centre and it is the subsequent investigation that will reveal this. The superior management will be in a position, after hearing from managers at each cost centre, to decide what should be done.

One important feature to recognize is that many of the variations and differences are not controllable and a weakness can be introduced if the cost-centre manager is made responsible for these.

Properly used the budgetary control system can highlight the areas of weakness in the operations of a company and show what should be done to correct any deficiencies before it is too late.

PART III The Role of Accounting and Finance

Chapter Fourteen

Structure of Taxation

The main taxes found in the United Kingdom are similar to those in most industrialized countries. Both direct and indirect taxes are present but the emphasis is on the direct tax with its link to income.

In the direct tax sector there are two main groups, the taxes on income and those on capital gains. The capital gains are subdivided into the gains made during the lifetime and on the sale or disposal of an asset and the taxing of the 'gains' made through saving during life and payable after death or when the capital assets are given away.

Both individuals and companies are liable and where possible the same rules for measuring are used, but for companies, which pay corporation tax, there are no taxes after death; a company, for this purpose has perpetual succession and should it close, any gains on the sale of the assets are charged.

Indirect taxes cover customs and excise duties, sales taxes and levies on leisure pursuits such as gambling. A business will only be involved in the last mentioned when the tax is levied on it as an operator.

Local taxes are collected from both individuals and companies through a system of property rating related to the occupier, not the owner.

There are pay-roll taxes under the guise of social security charges but these do not form a part of general taxation. They are used specifically to fund the state pensions, the health scheme, unemployment and sickness pay as well as redundancy payments. The burden of these on a business can be in the region of 10% of the payroll.

Indirect Taxes

These are under the control of HM Customs and Excise and for most of the levies the burden will fall initially on the user, then treated as a cost able to be passed on to the customer. Usually there is no need to disclose the amount of the tax in the price, so in most cases both the seller and purchaser along the chain of distribution seem to trade in ignorance of the amount. For this reason these taxes will be a profit and loss account item (although it may be further back in the trading or manufacturing account) rather than appearing in the balance sheet. There are a few exceptions when services and not goods are involved and any tax due appears as a creditor.

The exceptional tax is the Value Added Tax. This is a sales tax with the burden falling on the final consumer but where the government collects the tax by instalments along the chain of manufacture and distribution, instead of waiting to be paid in one amount when the retailer sells. It is really two taxes in one. There is the input tax paid by the purchaser on all trade purchases and an output tax which is applied as a percentage of the selling price when the goods are sold. The tax collected on the sales is paid over to the Customs and Excise at the end of a three month period less all the tax paid on the inputs.

This leaves the tax calculated on the added value payable at each stage so by the time the consumer purchases the goods or service only the tax on the value added at the retail stage remains to be paid over to complete the equivalent of a tax at the required percentage applied to the final sales value.

There are several advantages. The goods and services can be taxed according to their category and it is easy to apply different rates. If exports are involved and it is the intention to sell free of taxes, a zero rating is given which means that the sale is taxed at a nil rate but as it is considered taxed, the trader is able to recover all input tax charged to him. The effect is that the traders, before the exporter, do not have to worry about whether the goods are for export or not, while the exporter not only can recover the tax paid to date but can recover any tax paid on the incidental expenses in the business. This was very hard to do under the previous system of Purchase Tax.

144

Zero rating is used for essential goods.

Some goods or services are listed as exempt. Others are taxed at a higher rate where these come into a semi-luxury category, although in the United Kingdom the rates were consolidated back into the standard rate in 1979. If the supplies are not listed as liable to tax under one of these rates, the standard rate of tax applies.

As the trader can recover all tax paid on the inputs and merely passes over the tax collected on the outputs, there is no burden. The only burden is from the cost of recording both the inputs and the outputs and this, if incorporated into a simple system, need be neither time nor cost consuming.

With no tax burden, tax does not appear in the profit and loss (other than in the rare occasion when it is not recoverable). In the balance sheet, there will be a creditor for the balance due to the Customs and Excise for the current quarter.

Direct Taxes

These are under the control of the Commissioners of Inland Revenue who care for the income and capital taxes as well as the Oil Revenue Tax (levied on the income from oil of companies extracting from the North Sea), Development Land Tax and Stamp Duty. The last named is really an indirect tax but for historical reasons is still administered by the Inland Revenue who provide a valuation service which is sometimes needed to assess it. The Valuation branch is also used to value an estate after death and, every five years, revalue all property in the British Isles in connection with the values needed to levy the local rates.

Two other main departments exist. The COLLECTORS, whose function is to receive payment for tax, and the INSPEC-TORATE. It is these inspectors with whom the taxpayer has the most contact.

Every taxpayer is allocated to a tax district normally based on the place of business or employment. Within the district there are several inspectors whose task it is to receive the tax returns from the taxpayer, assess the amount of tax due and to communicate this to the taxpayer. Failure to inform the inspector of income or of capital gains is tax evasion and a criminal offence.

If the taxpayer, whether an individual or a corporation, does not agree with the assessment, the first appeal is to the inspector. Beyond him, most appeals are heard by the GENERAL COMMISSIONERS, although the taxpayer has the right to go to the SPECIAL COMMISSIONERS who are government employees with a highly specialized knowledge of taxation.

The General Commissioners are a panel of local men and women with certain land-holding qualifications. Normally they have no prior knowledge of tax but are guided by an accountant or solicitor, who acts as Clerk. Their task is to hear the appeal and to decide on the facts. On this decision they cannot be challenged other than in the case of fraud or negligence. They do interpret the law; and from this a further appeal by either the taxpayer or the inspector can go to the High Courts of Justice, then to the Court of Appeal and finally to the House of Lords.

If an appeal is made and the taxpayer wins, it is likely that the law on the point will be changed at the next Finance Act, to block the loophole found. However, tax legislation cannot be retrospective and as a result the taxpayer keeps the tax won and pays only from the date the law is passed.

Income tax

The main difference between Income Tax and Corporation Tax is not in the assessment but in the rates and method of payment. Income tax applies to individuals, partnerships and trusts; all others pay corporation tax.

Income tax is progressive with the rates rising in bands of taxable income and sometimes with the addition of a surcharge when the amount of unearned income exceeds a stated amount (unearned income refers to dividends, interest received and similar receipts). To mitigate the burden a series of reliefs are given in the form of personal allowance. The idea of these is to link the tax system to the individuals' social responsibilities.

As all forms of income cannot be taxed in a similar manner they are listed under what are termed SCHEDULES. In these the rules for measuring income are set out together with which expenses can be set against it. When the schedule becomes too comprehensive it has to be broken down into CASES. The schedules and their approximate contents are, for income derived from:

Schedule A: rents from the use of lands
       B: woodlands managed on a commercial basis
       C: government securities (UK and foreign) where paid through a UK paying agent
       D: —
  Case I trades and business
      II professions and vocations
     III interest not taxed at source
     IV overseas securities
      V overseas possessions
    VI not taxed elsewhere
       E: —
  Case I earnings when employee is resident in the UK
      II earnings in UK when the employee is not resident in the UK
    III earnings outside the UK on work performed outside the UK but where the employee is considered to be resident and remits back his earnings

With the exception of Schedule E most businesses can have the tax assessed under any schedule although Schedule C is restricted to the assessment made on the paying agent. This reflects that the aim of tax is to deduct it, where possible, as close to its source as it can be.

Tax on the business
Most businesses will be taxed for the main part of their activities under Schedule D, Case I. Under this case the starting point is the profit showing in the financial accounts. Adjustments are made to reduce it by those profits which are not allowed; these are specified in the law. Reduction is made for expenses able to be recovered through income in other schedules; and items, whether receipts or payments, of a capital nature are removed.

In the main the expenses which are 'wholly and exclusively' for the purpose of the business are allowed but, on the other hand, income from any business venture is brought in. There are many examples of whether or not trading has occurred that have been decided by the Courts.

One important expense which is charged to the profit and loss account and which must be added back (disallowed) is depreciation. This is not unjust but a means for the government to control or encourage capital expenditure.

Commercial depreciation could be deducted as an expense at whatever rate the management decided and if this were allowed for tax, there would be no uniformity existing. As a result the government have withdrawn depreciation and instead have substituted their own scheme of recovering the cost by CAPITAL ALLOWANCES.

In addition to producing uniformity, they are able to control the flow of investment and to direct it into certain areas. For example, there are no capital allowances given for office blocks or for shops. It does not stop a taxpayer buying a shop but only means that the expenditure incurred cannot be treated as an expense to be set against profit for tax purposes.

To encourage investment certain groups of assets obtain preferential rates. At present plant and machinery can be recovered in full against the tax in the year of purchase and new industrial buildings get an initial allowance of 50% in the first year, with the balance spread over the next twenty-five years.

If the business cannot take the full amount of the capital allowance in the year it is granted or the addition of the allowances turns the profit into a loss, they are not lost but are carried forward until there is sufficient profit to eliminate them. This must be done progressively and not by jumping a year or two; picking the year when the profits will be at their highest.

Losses were mentioned above and these, like capital allowances, are not lost. When a loss occurs there is no tax to pay in that year but the amount is carried forward to be set against the next profits. Sometimes, the following year also makes a loss and this merely increases the carry forward. This can go on without limit but they must be set against the first available profit.

In recent years another major relief has been introduced, this time to combat the effects of inflation. A feature of a trading account is that when the stock-in-trade at the end of the financial period is higher than the opening stock, the effect is to reduce the cost of sales and to increase the profit. As the tax paid is based on profits and the Inland Revenue must be paid in cash, the business has a double burden. It pays extra tax and also has to pay more for the replacement goods put into stock where the prices have risen through inflation. On the other hand, it is likely the prices being charged to the customer reflect not the new material prices but those from when the stock was purchased.

The government recognized this and brought in a scheme of STOCK RELIEF where the tax due on the increase arising from new cost is deferred. It is only allowed permanently after a period of six years. The reason for this being that, in this period, the prices could fall rather than rise or the business could run down the stock. When this occurs, any tax deferred becomes repayable.

Payment of tax
Payment of tax and sending of returns is based on the Income Tax Year. This runs from 6 April in one year to 5 April in the year following. The tax year 1979/80 is from 6 April 1979 to 5 April 1980.

This is not as illogical as it may seem. In the nineteenth century the tax year ended on the quarter day, 25 March, but at the end of the century to adjust the calendar eleven days were lost. To save supposed hardship to the taxpayer, the tax year was adjusted so that payment was made or the tax assessed as before.

The basis of assessment of business profits is on what is termed the previous year basis. Until the year has ended it is not possible to assess the tax, so unless the tax year is made to finish with the financial year, there must be a discrepancy. This is corrected by taking the profits of the financial year ending in the previous tax year as a basis for the tax in the current year.

To explain this by the use of dates. Assume the financial year of the business ended on 31 December 1978, which falls in the 1978/79 tax year. These profits would be used as the basis profits for the tax assessment on the business for the tax year 1979/80.

Again for historical reasons, the tax is payable in two instalments; 50% on 1 January in the tax year, that is, on 1 January 1980 and the balance on 1 July in the following tax year, that is, on 1 July 1980 which falls in the tax year 1980/81.

There are special rules for the opening of the business, when the taxpayer can take advantage of reduced payment, and for the closing when the Inland Revenue takes the advantage.

Corporation Tax

Apart from the rates of tax, the timing of the payment and some differences which occur due to the nature of a company, the trading profits are calculated under the same rules as for the individual and the partnership.

The rate of tax under corporation tax is not progressive; it is the same if the profits are £1 or £1 million. There is, however, a concession which has been introduced to ease the heavy burden of tax on the company which is able to make only a small amount of profit. Below a certain amount, at present £50,000, the rate of tax levied is 42%, 10% below the general rate.

This is not a 'slab' for if the profit exceeds this figure the whole is then subject to tax at the full rate of 52%. Obviously this could bring further hardship if the profits were to exceed the limit of £60,000 by a very small amount, so there is a sliding scale for profits below the lower limit up to £100,000 when the full rate comes in.

It goes by the name of the SMALL COMPANIES RATE which is misleading as it is not the size of the company which has effect but the amount of profit. If one of the giant industrial companies were to make profits below £60,000, they would be entitled to be taxed at 42%.

Payment of corporation tax

When corporation tax was first introduced into the United Kingdom in 1965, it was decided to rid this part of the system of a tax year not coinciding with a month end. The year runs from

1 April to 31 March in the year following and takes its name from the calendar year in which the major portion falls. The year from 1 April 1979 to 31 March 1980 is the tax year 1979.

This has significance in the setting of the tax rate as it is always announced in arrears, after the government are in a position to see how much tax has been raised to cover the expenditure in the previous year. In the budget proposals given in the April of 1980, the rate for 1979 will be announced.

Such an arrangement could cause chaos if applied to the present income tax structure with the preceding year but instead, a simple device is used to relate the company's financial year to the tax year and rate. Again assuming the company year ends on 31 December but this time in 1979 the proportion of the company profits which falls in 1978 tax year, that is from 1 January 1979 to 31 March 1979, will be taxed at the 1978 rate while the rest will be taxed at the 1979 rate.

If the rate does not change, either for the full rate corporation tax or for the small companies rate, there is no calculation to be made. If it does change then the profits are apportioned by time, as if those profits were earned evenly over the year.

Once the tax has been agreed, it becomes payable nine months after the end of the company's financial year or, if agreement with the inspector is later, one month after the assessment is made. Companies incorporated before 1965, when the corporation tax was introduced, are still entitled to pay their tax after the same time lag as when they were paying Income Tax and Profits Tax.

Distributions

A company paying a dividend is considered to be making a distribution of profit and so the dividend is not treated as a cost. This differs from interest payable on long-term loans such as debentures which are an expense in the profit and loss account and allowed for tax.

Between 1965 and 1973 the situation existed in which the company was taxed on its profits in the usual way and, out of the remainder, it paid the dividend. Before these dividends were paid over to the shareholder, Income Tax at the standard rate (not with the higher rates or surcharges) had to be deducted first and paid over to the Inland Revenue. This meant the shareholders were being taxed twice on the same profits made by the company.

This was felt to be unfair and created a tendency for companies not to distribute profits in order to save their shareholders tax. This happens as the undistributed profits are re-invested in the company causing the share value to rise; then when the share is sold only capital gains tax, which is at a much lower rate, is charged.

In 1973, the system of IMPUTATION was brought in. No longer was the shareholder taxed twice but on his own tax was given relief to the extent of the income tax on the company profits. This meant a loss in tax revenue and so the rates were increased to compensate. In broad outline, it works as follows.

When a company pays a dividend, it can pay it over to the shareholder without deduction of any tax, that is, at the full rate declared. At the same time it must pay over to the government a sum of money as ADVANCE CORPORATION TAX based on the amount of the dividend multiplied by a given fraction.

This is payable at the end of each quarter and compensates the government for the loss in the national cash flow when the system changed. It gives to the shareholders a tax credit showing how much tax the shareholder is imputed as having paid on the dividend.

The shareholder can use this either to get repayment, if he is below the tax threshold, or as a credit on the total tax he is due to pay.

Eventually the company is able to recover the advance payment against the corporation tax liability in the year in which the dividend was *paid*, not when it appeared in the accounts.

There is one concession, when a company receives a dividend from another company and on which the other company has had to pay over ACT, as it is known, the receiving company can deduct this amount of tax from its own payments of ACT. The effect is to tax the profits of a company once only, and make the tax payable by the company earning them.

Capital Gains Tax

Until now all the revenue referred to for tax has been earned from operating, but receipts often arise from capital transactions. Shares may be sold at a profit or other assets disposed of with a profit or a loss being made.

At one time these profits could be received free of tax but in 1965 a CAPITAL GAINS TAX was introduced. Although it applies to individuals the rules for deciding the amount of the gain or loss are the same for companies.

All gains from capital transactions are now liable for tax but in calculating the gain, all the expenses in acquiring the asset or disposing of it are allowed. If there is a capital loss this can be deducted from the capital gain but these losses, to be recovered, must wait for a gain as they cannot usually be used against profits of other kinds.

The rate of tax charged is somewhat lower than the income tax rate but unfortunately, due to inflation and a rate which has not changed since introduction in 1965, it has become a tax on wealth. The situation is that the value of money at the time of disposal differs from the value of money at the time the purchase was made. When the sale comes, the purchase value is in the pounds of, say, 1965, with the sale in the pounds of 1979, which have a much reduced purchasing power.

This factor is evident whether it is an individual or a company disposing of the asset.

When the company makes a capital gain, it is taxed under corporation tax but an adjustment is made by reducing the amount of the gain to make the effective rate of tax paid, the same as for an individual.

One other factor arises in the company, beyond the fact that unrelieved losses must usually be carried forward to the next gain, is that the small companies rate does not apply to capital transactions. They are all taxed at the full corporation rate.

Treatment in the accounts

Corporation tax for the year must appear in the appropriations section of the profit and loss account. It is not a cost but the share of the profit which goes to the government.

The tax due to be paid in the years coming will also be in the balance sheet under the general grouping of the current liabilities.

Another entry will often appear with the long-term liabilities as 'deferred tax'. This will contain any tax which is to be paid more than twelve months after the end of the financial year of the accounts, as well as any tax from the 'stock relief' deferred, and not up to the six-year period, after which the liability is cancelled.

It will also be adjusted for ACT but will not contain any amounts connected with tax which are not likely to be paid in the future. Until recently amounts arising from the taking of the full capital allowance in the first year were often included to bring in tax equalization. That is, there was an attempt to spread the tax so that the charge to the profit and loss account seemed to be level each year.

Close Companies

One of the extra burdens which have affected the United Kingdom tax scene over the last two decades has been the legislation on the close companies. Mainly it affects the smaller company and can have an adverse influence on the financial management of the companies concerned.

If a company has fewer than five participators, usually groups of shareholders and their families or the public holds less than 35% of the shares through the Stock Exchange, then it will be classed as 'close'. The effect is to enable the tax authority to enforce a distribution of profits over a certain amount or to tax the participators on an amount of dividend the Inland Revenue consider they should have received.

The level of distribution is fixed after taking in amounts that need to be retained in the business for future investment through the reserves.

Pay As You Earn (PAYE)

Employers are responsible, not only for their own payment of tax but they must deduct tax from employees before they make any payment to them. With the tax will be the contributions the employee makes for social security although the burden of this falls partly on the employer and is paid at the same time.

When deducting this tax, the employer acts as an agent for the government and has to account monthly for any amounts deducted. Fourteen days are allowed from the end of the tax month (ending on the 5th) for collections made in the previous month.

For each employee the company will receive a notice of coding. This is related to the amount of personal allowances the employee is to receive in the forthcoming year. When the code is related to the government supplied table this will show the 'amount of free pay' for the employee which can be deducted from the wage or salary before the tax due is payable. The free pay is the proportionate amount of the allowances due to the employee for the tax year to date.

By working on an accumulative basis it is possible to cater for employee sickness and varying wage receipts, with the object that, at the end of the tax year, the amount of tax deducted will be the earnings less the total allowances.

With a simple form which the employee takes from job to job incorporated into the system, if there is a change of employer, continuity of tax is maintained.

Employees working overseas
Recently a new concession was introduced for employees who had to spend time overseas on behalf of their companies.

Should they be out of the country for more than twelve months, there will be no United Kingdom tax to pay. If they are out for more than a total of thirty days in a year then the earnings due for the period they are out will be reduced by 25% before they are taxed.

On the other hand, should employees be out of the country for over a year and not be liable for tax, they will not upset their tax position if they come back for leave or for meetings. In this case they must not spend more than sixty-three days in the country in a year or more than one-sixth of the time overseas, if less than a year.

Overseas Tax

If an individual is domiciled, resident or ordinarily resident in the United Kingdom, he will be liable for tax on the whole of his global income and where appropriate on his world-wide possessions.

Domicile is the place to which he hopes and intends to return eventually. Residence is the place in which he resides, and ordinarily resident is where the residence is a part of everyday life.

A company is domiciled in the country in which the registered office is situated and if this is within the United Kingdom, it will be liable on its global earnings.

This situation can lead to difficulties, especially where trading is carried on in foreign countries who also like to tax profits earned within their boundaries. Sometimes this leads to a situation of double taxation with tax being due in both places.

To overcome this most countries enter into DOUBLE TAXATION AGREEMENTS in which the rules are laid down to eliminate one tax. In Britain the rule also exists for wherever there is no agreement in force, relief being given for the foreign tax paid.

The effect, for both the individual and the company, is that the UK taxpayer will pay the higher tax by being able to offset the tax paid against the UK liability. Should the situation be that the foreign tax is higher than the similar UK tax, then no repayment can be obtained.

The implication of double taxation is significant when international trade is involved.

Chapter Fifteen

External Sources of Capital

Capital for a company will come from either external sources or from the results of management policy and skills earning sufficient to provide funds for re-investment. At times, no matter how good the management is, extra capital will have to be brought in from the outside.

It may be that the project needing financing is too big for the company to use its own resources or an expansion has come too early in the life of the business for enough internal reserve to have been built up.

When there is the need to go outside, the correct source of capital must be approached for the needs of the business. Before a search commences, the management will have to be clear in their mind exactly why the capital is needed, how it is to be used and the benefits that will result from the extra investment. Details will be needed of the risk of a possible loss of investment and of the security that can be offered.

All this will be put together as a case for submission to potential investors to impress upon them the advantages they will obtain by investing with the company. The information will not be 'inflated' or distorted (in fact it must sometimes be prepared by independent accountants) but it will be constructed for the requirements of a particular source.

This will mean not only knowing the sources available but also knowing what the investor is looking for in a company.

Share Capital

The source of capital with the longest life expectancy is the share capital for, with the exception of the Redeemable Preference Share, it cannot be paid back without the company's

157

going into liquidation or special permission being obtained from the High Courts.

Two main classes exist, the ORDINARY SHARE and the PREFERENCE SHARE with many variations which contain elements of each.

The types of investors attracted to them will differ in their requirements. The holder of the preference share will want some security and this is given by the priority given to him over the ordinary shareholder in the payment of dividends. In return for this priority, which often is on a cumulative basis, he takes a fixed rate of dividend.

This fixed rate of dividend must not be confused with the fixed rate of interest coming from the loans to the company. The loan interest has to be paid in all circumstances but unless there are profits, no dividends can be paid at all.

The cumulative element arises in some preference shares with the feature that all arrears of dividend must be paid, whether relating to that year or previously, before any dividend can be paid to the holders of the ordinary shares.

For issues of the standard type of preference, there is not much public demand. This is due to the penal taxation system of the pre-1973 corporation tax with its element of double taxation coupled with inflation. This affects the fixed dividend. As it is based on a percentage of nominal capital, a rise in the money amount cannot be introduced to combat the falling value of purchasing power.

Some issues of preference shares are still made to institutions such as insurance companies, where for some types of the investment, only a steady income is required. Issues of this nature are usually placed.

Redeemable preference shares are slightly more popular although they also suffer from the inflation disadvantage. They can be used when extra capital is needed for a specific number of years but where the risk of an interruption in a cash flow does not allow the funds to be borrowed through a loan.

They would be suitable for financing a long construction project where the revenue flow might be held up by difficulties arising in the work. If this happened the company might not be able to pay the interest and the company could collapse. On the

External Sources of Capital

other hand, ordinary shares would not be suitable as when the contract finished and the initial outlay was recovered from the proceeds, the company would have surplus funds in its possession which it could not pay back but which still expect to receive some payment for being invested there.

The redeemable preference share fulfils all these requirements and offers the investor some recompense for the risk being taken.

With the preference share not being popular, it leaves the ordinary share as the most usual source of capital for general purposes. It may be issued for three reasons; to the general public or to a specialized institution as a new issue, as a rights issue when extra funds are required from existing shareholders, or as consideration (payment) for the assets taken over in a merger or company take-over situation. The last named is beyond the scope of this book but is a source of financing often used for the specific purpose for taking over another company.

Rights issues need some explanation. In some countries they are compulsory when further shares are to be issued. They represent an offer to the existing shareholders to subscribe for more shares in the company. The number of shares they have the right to subscribe for is given in proportion to the shares already held and as an inducement the price is fixed below market price.

Shareholders have a choice, they can either put in the extra funds and reap the benefits of the increased capital or they can sell their rights to the highest bidder and keep the proceeds.

As the majority of shares in the United Kingdom and other highly industrialized countries are held by the institutions, the success of such an issue will depend upon whether these holders can be persuaded to invest further.

This leaves an issue of shares for cash to the public and in the United Kingdom, at present, the most popular method is by placing.

There are several methods of making an issue to the public. The company can arrange to issue the prospectus, giving details about itself, and then handle all the applications and subsequently allot the shares. Alternatively, it can arrange for an issuing house to do this for a fee and save on the immense administrative burden an issue brings with it. Most of these are Offers for Sale where in practical terms the issuing house buys the shares from the company and sells them on to the public.

The other method is by placing. In this either an issuing house, a broker or a merchant bank arranges for blocks of the shares in the issue to be placed with investors. These are usually institutions such as insurance companies, pension funds and trusts. Later, as a part of the institution's normal trading pattern, the shares will be sold on through the recognized channel of the Stock Exchange, assuming they have obtained a listing. Sometimes where shares are not listed, placing is still carried out but the subsequent sales are not so easy to achieve.

Placing is used more in the United Kingdom, at present, than the other issuing method, probably due to the concentration of funds in the hands of the institutions rather than as private savings.

These institutional funds are indirectly the savings of the public through the widespread compulsory pension contributions, the insurance premiums collected or the purchase of units in the unit trusts (in certain countries known as mutual funds).

When raising capital through shares, this must not be at a discount, that is, issued below the nominal price, but there is nothing to stop them being issued at a premium. In fact it is rare, other than in the small private company where the capital comes from the directors in the main, to find modern shares issued at par.

For new introductions the financial advisors of the company will calculate the price they think the market will bear. For subsequent issue of shares already quoted the price will be fixed, again usually by the advisors, at a level it is believed all the company shares will sink to after the new issue has been made.

The theory is simple and an example of a subsequent issue will show this. The existing shares are standing at 105 pence for a 25 pence share and after the issue of the new shares the share is likely to drop to 75 pence. The new capital the company needs is £75,000. If the company were to issue at par, that is, at 25 pence a share it would have to issue 300,000 shares and the lucky persons who were allotted those shares would, if they had any financial sense at all, sell immediately and make a profit of 50 pence per share.

The company, in turn, would have to pay a dividend on the 300,000 shares into eternity while the profit was taken by holders who stayed only a very short time. As there is no reason why the company should not take advantage of the profit, after all it was their good management and trading that has put the price above par, the issue price becomes 75 pence and there is a need for only 75,000 shares to be issued and serviced with dividend. The rest of the amount, above the nominal value, is held by the company free of dividend needs, although it does belong to the equity holder as a capital reserve and cannot be distributed as dividend.

Debentures

A debenture is strictly a document in evidence of a loan but in modern usage it has become the loan document where security is involved. If there are a series of debentures or because the debenture is to be held by many people in the public, the control is put into the hands of trustees.

When the issue is made to the public and it is expected the loan will be dealt in, as are shares, it is called MORTGAGE DEBENTURE STOCK, DEBENTURE STOCK, LOAN STOCK, SUBORDINATED LOAN STOCK and, as a more recent innovation, CONVERTIBLE LOAN STOCK. In most cases, the name is indicative of either the security given for the loan or the main terms in the contract of borrowing. The subordinated loan can be paid back only after certain other loans have been returned to the lenders whilst the holders of the convertibles can change their loans into the shares of the company at a predetermined date and ratio.

As a form of long-term capital, loans are advantageous both to the company and to the holder. Because security is offered a lower rate of interest is paid by the company and unlike shares, they can be paid back. For the lender, there is security which can be taken and realized if the company fails to fulfil its obligations under the terms of the loan. This is normally failure to pay the interest when it becomes due.

The cost of loan capital and the type of security offered will be discussed in a later chapter.

Some Sources for Shares and Debentures

Most of the funds available come from the institutions rather than from the public, and these have been mentioned earlier, with one notable exception.

The exception is a newcomer to the scene, the NATIONAL ENTERPRISE BOARD. This is a government-funded body which takes shares in public corporations with the aim of giving the government ownership of shares in industry and also providing large sums of money through shares or debentures which could not be provided through the normal market issue processes. This could be because the sum is too large or the market conditions are such that there is not the amount being offered for investment generally.

Larger companies can turn, also, to the FINANCE CORPORATION FOR INDUSTRY(FCI) which is a part of an investment body known as FINANCE FOR INDUSTRY. This was set up by the Bank of England and the Clearing Banks as a way to invest in industry, a thing they were not able to do directly.

For most companies, where they are smaller, their source of finance is with an associated company, the INDUSTRIAL AND COMMERCIAL FINANCE CORPORATION. This covers industry and commerce in general and has other associates to provide finance in specialized areas such as agriculture or development.

Recently, to help to satisfy some of the demand for this type of finance in the smaller company, the insurance industry set up EQUITY FOR INDUSTRY as another method for them to invest their premium income.

Some of the pension funds, together with merchant banks, also have schemes through trust companies to provide long term finance.

Merchant banks have been giving this service for many years although their objective was not long-term investment. By taking shares in a small company with potential, in return for the injection of capital, they hope with the management guidance they provide, to expand it to the stage when the shares can be listed on the Stock Exchange. The merchant bank then sells to the public and takes its profit.

Medium-term Capital

Not all companies need long-term funds, only help for a few years to become established or to finance a project. Debentures from insurance companies are often arranged to meet this need but some specialist agencies are useful.

Many regional schemes are operated with the primary intention of attracting industry to their part of the country. THE HIGHLANDS AND ISLANDS DEVELOPMENT AUTHORITY in Scotland and the WELSH DEVELOPMENT AUTHORITY in Wales are in this category although sometimes, as with the government Department of Trade and Industry, the assistance takes the form of a grant.

For the very small company with a workforce of under twenty, loans of up to £30,000 can be obtained through the COUNCIL FOR SMALL INDUSTRIES IN RURAL AREAS (CoSIRA) or the equivalent agencies outside England.

Lastly, if there is a product which needs to be exploited there are loans and grants to be obtained from the NATIONAL RESEARCH AND DEVELOPMENT CORPORATION (NRDC) but the main part of their payment in return is through a royalty charged on the sale of the goods.

Most of the loans need some security to reinforce them.

For the very large company, one which can obtain a government guarantee, or a government agency, medium term funds can come from a loan raised on the Euro-market. This will be in a foreign currency and comes from several international bankers lending out the funds deposited with them. The amount of the loan is usually in millions of pounds and the term up to seven years.

Short-term Sources

When borrowing in the short-term most companies turn to the bank overdraft and for many this is the only source available. The security is a floating charge (using all the assets as a collateral) or, for very small companies, the personal guarantee of the directors.

It has the great disadvantage of needing to be reviewed every six months by the bank and should the government decide to impose credit restrictions there is always the risk it will not be renewed.

In recent years, to overcome this failing, the banks have offered term loans of two or three years. The fact that they cannot be called in ahead of maturity, excluding by default, means that companies can plan the best use. Some of these short loans can be obtained through the finance houses either termed as a loan or as an acceptance credit.

This method refers to the practice of the borrower accepting to pay, at a stated date in the future, the sum involved and if they do not, the payment can be enforced through the Courts.

Hire-purchase can be used as a source of finance with the repayments spread over a two or three year period. Often this can be used to allow the asset to be acquired earlier and then to earn its own cost from profits.

In some industries, it is possible to arrange stocking finance, usually through the banks. If there is a seasonal problem needing a large increase in stock at a certain time and with other periods on low stock levels, the injection of temporary capital allows the minimum of permanent capital which would otherwise be idle for most of the year.

Nearly all the short-term capital involves the financing of working capital and is suited to support the fluctuations which occur in this. Other than hire-purchase, to use short-term capital as fixed capital is a great risk to the survival of the business.

One area of the working capital has been omitted, the use of the debtors. Often substantial sums of money are locked up which could be used to buy further materials and expand. A profit although taken, in accountancy terms, as soon as the invoice is issued, cannot be spent in cash until the customer has paid.

To use this money, it is possible to sell invoices to certain finance houses who, for interest charged, advance a certain proportion immediately and pay the balance, usually as low as 15%, when the customer does pay. This is INVOICE DIS-COUNTING and the 'seller' chooses which invoices can be used. As he must pay back any sums advanced in the event of failure by the customer to pay (the advance is said to be with recourse), he must make this choice carefully.

A more sophisticated system came to the United Kingdom from the United States of America in the first half of the 1960s. This is INVOICE FACTORING. It is an on-going operation and it is not unusual for the factor to insist on a contract to use his services for at least one year.

All the invoices must be presented to the factor, good and doubtful, although there is no obligation to draw the advance of money. Should the customer not pay, there is no recourse, the factor standing the loss and because of this, it is the factor who carries out the debt-collecting and chasing. This creates a saving for the company as the factor is effectively keeping the sales ledger.

As a form of releasing working capital for expansion, this is very effective but inclined to be expensive.

Chapter Sixteen

Raising Capital Internally

The policy of most companies is not to distribute all of the profit as dividend but to retain a portion for re-investment in the business.

This is not just a whim of the management for pressures to do this come from the shareholders, the stock markets and the advisors. It is a good and sound practice.

Several reasons are put forward, other than that the government of the day may have a restriction in force as to how dividends can be distributed. The foremost is to ensure that the capital of the company is maintained in real and not just in money terms.

When many assets were purchased, money was worth more than it is today and to replace the present asset by one similar would cost a lot more money. The extra needed for replacement should come from the profits generated by the use of the original asset, otherwise the management will be losing some of the capital. The depreciation held back from the profit each year is sufficient to cover and maintain at the first level. The capital generated from the profit brings it up to the present level necessary.

A further reason why there is a great deal of re-investment, at least in the United Kingdom, is taxation. Previously the system discriminated against a distribution and even now as the rate of tax on investment income is higher than on the profit made on the sale of the shares, so re-investment is a service to the shareholders.

If the distribution is not made, the funds which are retained will undoubtedly be put to use, first to purchase new assets and then to use those assets to generate further profit. Both of these things will make the company more valuable and, correspondingly, the price of the shares will rise.

This retention of profit is the best and often the cheapest source of capital a company has available.

It is the best as, in raising it, the company does not have to suffer the full rigour of an examination into its affairs nor is it likely to suffer from external economic factors on timing. Often when the capital is needed the market has not sufficient funds available to meet the demands.

It is cheap as the company does not have to pay the costs of raising it. However, contrary to belief, it is not free.

If shareholders are going to leave their money as extra capital in the company they will expect to be recompensed for doing it. They will expect the money to earn, at least, the same return as the original funds they have invested. Should the return they are getting now be below the rate expected from similar investment opportunities with a similar amount of risk involved, they will expect to get that higher rate.

Of course, the directors could decide to keep all the profit. Then, not only are they likely to be removed, but the shareholders will show their displeasure by selling their shares and buying other shares or investing to get the return they expect.

Sources of Capital

Not all the profit for re-investment comes from a greater volume of trading; much of it can come from more efficient internal operating.

Obviously, much of this can be by a better use of labour or by cutting down the wastage on materials, better buying and a more effective sales force, not forgetting the other consumer of profits, the administration departments.

Often these savings are small against the savings which can be made from the stocks of raw materials or finished goods. The policy should be to keep as little stock as possible 'on the shelves' and to let others keep it instead.

Much can be learned from the motor car assembly industry. They have a system with the minimum safety stock being held and daily deliveries of components. Of course, until the goods are delivered, they do not become liable to pay and a great deal of capital becomes free for other uses.

167

Even such a simple solution as going through the stock to dispose of items not likely to be used in the next few years will save. One American company used to divide its stock-holding into three: current, slow moving and obsolete. The last two had to be justified before they were retained.

Disposing of finished goods may prove to be harder but one solution is to ship out to customers on a 'sale or return' basis or even on extended terms. With larger items, such as in the agricultural machinery industry, much space is saved and consequently capital does not have to be tied up.

A careful watch on the debtors is another rewarding internal source of capital. A good credit control system brings the money in earlier and reduces the amount of working capital needed. If customers know there is a system in operation which will chase the laggardly payers, they usually pay. If they had been three months overdue, then the interest paid on extra capital needed to service the debt probably takes away the profit on the sale.

Many companies give discounts to induce payment but cash discounts are expensive and it has been said that the best policy is to take all possible discounts but not to give any.

Two types of discount exist. The trade discount which is given either on account of the size of the order or on the status of the customer. It is a reduction on the selling price and does not vary whether the customer pays or not. The cash discount is an inducement to pay within a certain time limit.

If a $2\frac{1}{2}$% cash discount is offered for payment by the end of the month the cost on an annual basis, if there is a regular monthly amount, is 30% in money terms or as a real rate of interest it is worth about 33%. When this is given on sales, it is likely it would be cheaper to borrow the sum outstanding at any time from the bank as an overdraft.

Accounting for the Internal Capital

Internally raised capital, like its counterpart from outside, has to appear in the balance sheet. If it has come from inside, instead of being passed out to shareholders as dividends, it represents dividends not taken and must then belong to the equity shareholders. It will appear, in the balance sheet, with the worth of shareholders under the name of 'Reserves'.

To the casual reader of the accounts, this name probably leads to more misunderstanding than any other term. Most people ask, if these are reserves, why cannot the money shown there be used when the company is in trouble? If, instead of reserves, these were termed 'Internally Raised Capital', all of that would be avoided.

The answer to where has all the money gone is quite simple. When the profit was generated, and for this purpose it is assumed that cash for the sales and purchases was made immediately, it went to restore the working capital used to make the product, then to pay the tax and finally to pay a dividend. Any cash left over, rather than being left idle in the bank, was used up to purchase further assets for the expansion of the business.

In the balance sheet the assets will be increased and to balance this, these funds will appear as a future liability to the shareholders. This means that if those assets are sold in the future, the proceeds are acknowledged as belonging to the shareholders. The cash in the reserves has been spent earlier and cannot be used again.

To complete the mechanics of double-entry, any transfers to the reserves will also be shown in the appropriations section of the profit and loss account as it is a disbursement of profit.

Chapter Seventeen

Debt, Gearing and Cost of Capital

In the earlier chapter shares were looked at in some detail and the various sources of capital were discussed. Other than the shares and the re-invested profits most of the sources involve borrowing, in one form or another.

No mention was made of the security that must be offered or of the cost to the business that must be incurred through the lender wanting a reward – a reward to cover the use of the money and also to compensate for the risk involved.

The basic security the lender has in a company is given by the shares. He will wish to see a substantial amount put into the company as share capital and will most likely find the larger part of the fixed assets to have been bought out of the amounts put into the business by the shareholders, either as cash or by way of retained earnings.

With the shares contributing a large part, the lender will know he will take priority over them in the event of the need to recover the sum lent. Shares are always the last to be repaid when a company ceases to trade, the assets are sold and the liabilities settled.

That security is not enough and the lender will expect more, although usually the rate of interest will be linked to security and also to the size of the company. The better the security and the larger the size of the company, the lower will be the rate.

The best backing security of all is a mortgage on property. It does not really differ from a mortgage on a private house other than where the debenture is held by more than one person or organization there have to be trustees appointed for convenience.

If there are several debenture holders and the borrowing company fails to meet its obligations under the contract to borrow, all the holders have to agree before action can be taken. If some of these are in distant parts of the world or some think the remedial action to be too drastic, nothing can be done. By appointing trustees, who are empowered to act on behalf of all the trustees, without having to consult them, action can be taken very quickly and the security is protected.

Many of the trustees appointed, at present, are the trust departments or companies belonging to the clearing or merchant banks.

Taking a mortgage debenture has one major drawback which, when property is involved, is not serious. Before the company can dispose of the security, even if it is to be replaced with another even better, the authority of the debenture holders must be obtained. This precludes the use of the mortgage for assets other than property. In its place a debenture, secured by a floating charge, has been introduced.

Under the terms of this, the company is able to continue to trade normally, buying and selling its assets of all types. Then if things go wrong and the company fails to meet its obligations, it loses this power to trade and all the assets pass into the control of the debenture holders, as the security for the floating charge, to be sold in repayment of the sum borrowed and for interest outstanding. Any assets left after the debenture holders have been satisfied must be returned to the company but usually when this stage is reached, it is only a preliminary step to the winding-up.

In recent years a further form of borrowing has been introduced by the very large companies with a first-class reputation and good asset backing. This is a debenture without any formal security.

Unsecured debentures rank on a level with the trade and any other creditors, and this form of borrowing is really on name.

It has been extended still further by its use when money is borrowed on the Euro-market. These lendings originate from the money in the international banking system and are usually for sums of millions of pounds. Where possible the bankers, through whom this money is channelled, like to obtain the guarantee of the government of the country in which the borrower is registered, but this is likely to be restricted to the

171

nationalized industries, the government agencies and the quasi-government organizations.

Redemption of Debentures

No mention has been made, so far, of the redemption of debentures. Unlike shares which, other than the Redeemable Preference, cannot be paid back, a loan can be repaid.

Several choices are open to the company. At the end of the term, repayment is to be made in cash, with or without an additional premium. This can be in cash from profits or from a new issue of shares or debentures. If the articles of association permit, the debentures can be purchased on the open market and cancelled. Alternatively they may be kept to be re-issued if more cash is required later.

Finally, if the procedure was allowed for in the original contract to borrow, the redemption can be by drawings. A certain proportion of the total loan is to be repaid each year and owners of the debentures to be prematurely retired are found by putting all the numbers of the debentures on issue into a box and drawing out the unlucky few. The owners of the numbers drawn do not have the option to refuse to take the repayment.

Cost of Debentures

As has been stated the cost of debentures to a company depends upon the risk the lender considers he is taking reduced by the security offered. The amount available for borrowing will depend on the market rate for lending at similar risk.

From the company's point of view, this is a very cheap manner in which to obtain money, due to the taxation situation. The gross rate is fixed, according to the market, but when the company pays the interest it is able to treat this as a cost to the business and as a charge in the profit and loss account allowable for tax. The result is that the effective rate is considerably less than the apparent or nominal rate. The following shows this. A company has £350,000 issued as 10% debenture stock needing £35,000 to be charged each year to the profit and loss account. With the rate of corporation tax at 52% and with the whole amount allowed as an expense, the true cost to the company is £16,800 (£35,000 minus tax of 52% = £18,200) or 4.8% of the sum borrowed.

This calculation ignores the effect of inflation. Loans are not indexed so the amount to be repaid is in the money terms of the amount originally borrowed. When this is put into purchasing power the effect on a medium or long term loan is to reduce the true rate even further. Unless inflation is in double figures the effect on the short term loan is very small.

Gearing

With the cost of borrowed money so much lower than the cost of funds obtained through shares, the question can be asked as to why a company does not maintain the statutory minimum limit for shares and borrow its requirements.

The answer is risk. As mentioned above the lender likes to see some asset backing to allow him to be repaid should things go wrong. The other part of the risk is the inability to be able to pay the interest as it falls due and as this must be paid on time. The earnings of the company must be large enough to ensure this.

An additional benefit and a characteristic of a company with a high debt content is that when the interest has been paid any surplus goes to the ordinary shareholders. As the interest is fixed, then a small increase in the profit after paying the interest gives a large increase in the amount of earnings per share.

A further effect of the need to obtain high earnings is on the stability of the company. The need to earn the interest usually leads to excessive drive and the obtaining of 'quick' profits on the basis 'to-day we are here, tomorrow we are likely to go'.

On the other hand the company which has no debt is suffering in two ways. Although it is very stable, it is having to pay very dearly for the money invested by the shareholders. They expect a far higher return from the investment than the debenture holders, as they have no security, but when they receive the money it does not suffer tax nor can it be allowed as an expense for tax by the company.

The other way in which the shareholders are caused to suffer is that in the absence of debt the funds invested are not able to work to the full nor can the full amount of funds be obtained. As has been said, the effective rate for borrowing is low and as the interest rate is fixed any surplus belongs to the shareholders, so the more debt that is included the greater is the share-out for the holders of the equity.

The relationship between the debt and the equity capital is monitored through the GEARING.

This is the ratio of the debt and other fixed interest capital to the total capital. If the debt exceeds half of the total capital the company is said to be 'highly geared' while a low-geared company exists when the equity is greater. In the United Kingdom the tradition was not to allow the debt to exceed the 50% level but now, with the cheapness of debt, this 'barrier' is being broken.

The ratio is used in assessing the vulnerability and stability of a company as well as making a quick check to see if it has an ability to carry more debt.

Uses of Capital

To get the balance right the company has to take different types of capital for different purposes and the successful company will have a mixture of all types to give the best result and to keep the cost at the best level for the full employment.

Long-term assets need financing from the long-term capital. This is better to be in shares although for a part 'irredeemable' debentures are a possibility. These debentures are only repayable at the choice of the company, unless there is a breach of the terms and conditions of the loan. Even then shares are better as the assets concerned can be used as a collateral for other borrowing.

Some long-term capital from shares should be used to finance a part of the working capital. The 'hard-core' part which never varies.

Major projects and expansions which are likely to be self-financing, even in the long term, can get their funds from the medium term capital (up to fifteen years), preferably by debt but in certain circumstances from redeemable preference shares.

Acquisition of further assets can be financed from medium term debt when the cash flow is sufficient to cover both the payment of interest and the repayment. The most popular source here is the hire-purchase contract.

Medium term loans are also obtained when the assets to be obtained consist of another company. Whether this is possible depends on the strength of the purchasing company and the earning potential of the company taken over.

Working capital financing causes problems. The underlying base needs long-term finance and on expansion there should be an increase in this to ensure there is no overtrading. However, it is also possible to finance a part from medium term capital.

Short-term capital should be left to equalize the fluctuations in the working capital and to counter the emergencies which occur in the financing of even the best run business.

Cost of Capital

If a company is going to obtain extra funds, it is important that it knows how much they are going to cost. One reason for this is that should the funds be used for a new project, the potential earnings should be more than the cost of capital or it will not be worth starting.

Whether the average cost of capital or the cost of the capital needed for the project is used, becomes a matter of choice and debate.

It can be said that the incremental cost (the cost of the extra) should be used as then the potential of the new venture can be measured. On the other hand, capital is hardly ever used exclusively for financing a specific project. Some of the extra borrowing may find its way to the rest of the business but more likely some of the capital needed will be supplied from existing sources.

If the average cost is used, this is nearly always weighted to reflect the influence of each type. In the example below a company has £300,000 in ordinary shares on which it is expected by the shareholders to pay dividends at an annual rate of 20%. There are £250,000 in reserves which can be said to cost a similar amount. Then there is £350,000 in loan stock, with a coupon of 10%. To keep a comparison the loan stock interest is taken at pre-tax.

Type	Amount	Proportion		Cost	Weighted Average
	£			%	%
Ordinary shares	300,000	33.3	×	20	6.66
Reserves	250,000	27.8	×	20	5.56
Loan stock	350,000	38.9	×	10	3.89
	900,000				16.11

One use of the weighted average cost would be as a 'cut-off' rate. Unless a project could earn more than this amount, it should not be undertaken.

Chapter Eighteen

Controlling Working Capital

Planning of capital covers the use to be made of both the working capital and the fixed capital in the form of assets. Both are equally important.

The planning of the fixed capital is dealt with in the following chapter, while this chapter concentrates on the working capital.

In some ways this is more difficult to manage as it is continuously fluctuating and many of the parts interact with each other. For example, a growing debtors list will reduce the cash and, in turn, it will become more difficult to pay the creditors.

Management of Stocks

A considerable amount of money is tied up in the stock and it has to be realized that the shorter the time it is on the shelves the quicker will the profits be earned.

This means that its stay should be short and there should be no overstocking and, unless it is essential, the company should not carry the little amount extra just in case there is a shortage at some time in the future. The funds tied up in the extra could most probably earn much more elsewhere and not be a cost burden.

Stocks are maintained for three main purposes; for the raw materials, etc. to be ready when wanted for the planned production, to cover the interval between the placing of an order and the delivery and for taking advantage of an economically low price through a bulk buy or something of that nature.

Sometimes, in inflationary times high stocks are held to counter the rapid rise in the cost of replacements.

Calculations must be done to ensure the benefit arising from holding the stock does not outweigh the charge for the capital.

Minimum stocks must be fixed with this in mind but care must be taken to ensure the stock does not run out as the cost of this will be high. Levels must be set to give normal production for the delivery time. The practice is to set a minimum stock, a re-order level and a re-order quantity. Formulae exist for this to be done in a quasi-scientific way.

In these days of rapidly advancing technology, one of the risks in stocking is that the stock will become redundant through obsolescence. This is very probable when the stock is carried as spare parts for servicing products sold some years before. The task here is to be resolute in disposing of many of the parts, even as scrap, when the demand is likely to be one every two or three years. It will be financially beneficial to order one new when the need arises, although it may have to be made specially.

Such a policy not only allows the further stock to be purchased but also cuts down the cost of stocking. It releases valuable space and does not need the services of the stores to care for it.

Debtors

Keeping down the amount outstanding in the debtors relies entirely upon a firm policy and a routine which is adhered to, in spite of the fears of the sales staff. If a debtor is persistently overdue and for a considerable period, it is better to lose the customer and find a new one. Not only is the cash flow disrupted but the company incurs the additional charges in sending reminders and possibly legal charges in obtaining the collection.

Controlling the debtors starts when the order is accepted. Before it is, a credit check should be carried out on the customer through credit reports and other sources. In this it is better to use external agencies, as to follow the common practice of asking for trade references is only a paper exercise. No debtor is going to give a referee unless his account with him is perfect.

It may pay at this stage to insure the debt, for the insurers will then need to approve all orders and due to the wealth of information coming into their hands they are able to set very realistic limits. If collections are to be made without trouble, instructions need to be sent to staff about requirement to get top management sanction before order limits can be exceeded.

Once the order is approved and shipped, one of the cheapest ways to get in the money is to invoice promptly. In these days, with the extensive use of computers, in the larger businesses there is a very strict timetable to deal with all matters. If the invoice is not presented in time it will miss the batch for payment in that month and will have to wait until the following payments go through.

In the United Kingdom, it is still customary to send out monthly statements. These are copies of the sales ledger account held and they serve as a check on whether the customer has received all invoices and whether some are held up in the authorization process. Even with the coming of the mini-computers the statement will have its use and also its abuse when customers fail to pay on the grounds that they have not received the latest statement. Statements should be out in the first week of the month following the month when the sale was made.

If the customer still does not pay, a rigid routine should come in so that, by the time it is three or four months overdue, legal steps are being taken for collection. If these steps are not taken, especially after they have been threatened, customers will take longer and longer credit and the profit will be eaten away by having to finance the debt for the extra time.

Control is exercised as well, through the debtors budget which takes the budgeted sales and calculates the inflow by reference to the planned credit terms to be offered.

To make sure the laggardly payers do receive their correct treatment, a further check is made by preparing an aged schedule of debt. Amounts outstanding by each customer are analysed by months and it can be seen very easily where there are areas which should be investigated.

Creditors

Control over the creditors is not as vital in the short run as the control over the debtors but there is a need to attempt to keep the pattern of the budget in line with the plan as it was developed from the production and the purchasing budgets.

While slow payments are helpful to the liquidity position, they can have an effect on the profitability of the company. In the first place, if the goods purchased are not standard and ordered from catalogues, it is likely that the supplier will recover the interest he pays on the debt by putting up the price. Where it is a catalogue item, the price will still go up, as a recovery of the increase in the overheads caused by the extra financing charges.

In the second place, if a customer is slow to pay, the supplier is not likely to be eager to supply and should the ordering firm need the goods in a hurry, it may find that this cannot be done and they have to wait for the standard delivery.

The rule should be to take the full credit terms agreed and not to overdo using another's trade credit as short-term finance.

Cash

Management of cash is essential. The uncontrolled spending whether on the capital account or for items within the working capital, without having a planned inflow against it, is a sure recipe for disaster.

The problem lies in the fact that cash involves all aspects of the business and, although from the profit and loss account can be seen the profitability, this does not indicate that a company can pay its bills when they become due. There is a vast difference between examining a situation on the basis of when the transactions are taken into account, that is recording when the sales are made or when the invoices for purchases are recorded, and studying the actual timing of the receipts and payments.

The planning for this is done through a cash budget constructed to show the timing of the cash coming inwards and the expenditure, whether it is to do with operating or connected with the sale or purchase of assets.

For planning purposes, it is prepared at the same time as the other budgets, on an annual basis with the control periods in months. For practical purposes, especially if the funds are low and need a tight control, this can be broken down, as the year progresses, into weekly or even daily budgets.

A specimen is shown in fig. 24. One feature to note is how the sales receipts are constructed. The sales are booked and the expected payment pattern developed to show the time lag. From experience or statistics the proportion of debtors paying after a certain time can be found and incorporated.

Similar treatment can be introduced to reflect the credit period taken from the suppliers and sometimes for the payment of expenses.

When preparing such a budget, it must be remembered it is not 100% accurate – it cannot be – and so certain constraints are necessary. For example, if salaries are paid on the last day of January, then this is booked as January expenditure, while a receipt the next day will have to be taken as February. In fact, there could be two or three days variation, but this has to be ignored.

A useful additional feature which will come from the budget is the revelation of the times when the cash position may be critical or, under happier circumstances, as a surplus.

In the planning stage, it may be possible to see the effect of re-positioning some of the payments or to be warned of approaching troubles and so arrangements are made in good time. Money obtained by advanced planning is usually cheaper than emergency money.

It may be that the cash budget will show a surplus of funds and then steps can be taken to make short term investments, to allow them to make some profit and not be idle. Such surpluses can be put with a bank on deposit or, if large enough, with a finance house. Other opportunities could be the purchase of Treasury Bills, short-term Government Securities and other 'near cash' investments. Investments can be made for

	Jan	Feb	Mar	Apr	May	Jun
Receipts						
Cash Sales	£4,550	4,300	4,100	5,200	6,000	6,550
Credit Sales 1	1,300	950	850	1,000	1,450	1,700
Credit Sales 2	2,650	2,600	1,900	1,700	2,000	2,900
Redemption of Investments				10,000		
	8,500	7,850	6,850	17,900	9,450	11,150
Payments						
Purchases	4,300	3,700	3,450	3,550	4,750	5,550
Wages/Salaries	3,850	3,750	3,800	4,150	4,600	6,200
Rates				550	750	
Other Expenses	750	750	750	750		750
Purchase of Assets					8,000	
	8,800	8,200	8,000	9,000	18,000	12,500
Surplus/Deficiency	(300)	(350)	(1,150)	8,900	(8,550)	(1,350)
Closing Bank Balance (opening £2,950)	2,650	2,300	1,150	10,050	1,500	150

Notes. 1. Credit sales are paid ⅓rd in month following month of sale and ⅔rds in month following.
2. Purchases are paid for in month following month in which invoice was received.

Fig. 24   XYZ Ltd., cash budget for period 1 January–30 June, 19—.

periods as short as seven days and in the large company the size of funds involved can make this type of cash management worthwhile.

It may seem to be trivial but in practice, most companies have a cash surplus, or if working on overdraft, a bettering of the cash position in the middle of each month. This arises from the receipt of most sales proceeds from debtors in the first week, followed by low expenditure with the exception of wages, until the suppliers are paid at the end of the month.

Flow of Funds Statement

A flow of funds statement is a recent innovation into the accounting reports which are presented to management and the shareholders. It goes under several names, all amounting to the same; cash flow statement, funds flow, and sources and application of funds statement.

They all show the same information – where the company received its finance from in the financial year and how it used it. Whereas the reports connected with the cash budgeting look in detail at the cash and are concerned with timing, these statements take an overall view of the movements of the funds.

In the last few years the listed companies in the United Kingdom have had to produce these statements as a part of the information for shareholders. A Statement of Standard Accountancy Practice (number 10 in the series) makes this mandatory.

The idea is simple. A profit and loss account looks only at the operating of the company and gives an analysis of the revenue and the expense (the costs). It does not analyse the monies the company uses nor does it incorporate any capital transactions. On the other hand it does bring in transactions which are only book entries involving no external movement at all.

There is no need to go further and this is found in the statement. The movements are found in the analysis of two consecutive balance sheets after adjustments have been made to eliminate the non-cash items such as depreciation and provisions for deferred tax.

A specimen of a flow of funds statement is found in fig. 25.

Sources of Funds	£000
Group profit before tax	4,162
Currency gains (on translation)	40
Depreciation	1,414
Book value (net) of fixed assets sold	88
Generated from operations	5,704
Sale of shares in subsidiary	86
Shares issued for acquisition of subsidiary	4,238
Plant Lease adjustments	768
	£10,796
Application of Funds	
Fixed assets additions	2,284
Subsidiary formation charges	8
Increase in stocks	3,930
Increase in debtors	2,688
Increase in creditors	(4,104)
Funds used for operations	4,806
Acquisition of subsidiary companies	4,388
Taxation	358
Dividends	618
	£10,170
Increase in bank position	£ 626

Fig. 25   XYZ Ltd. and its subsidiaries. Group sources and application of funds statements for year ending 31 May 19——.

The statement, for use with the published accounts, balances the sources and the application, but for internal use the statement can be rearranged to give the increase in the working capital during the year or to show how much deficit was present in the same area. By analysing the change in the working capital it is possible to see exactly which sector contributed to the result.

It is also possible to use the statement with projected figures as a planning device to give the effect on the working capital of the proposed operating. From this any shortage can be foreseen and where possible plans made to remedy this deficit.

Chapter Nineteen

Capital Budgeting and Capital Appraisal

As it is necessary to plan the operations of a company and the cash movements, so must the expenditure on assets and capital projects be dealt with in the same way.

There is a difference, the plans need to cover a longer period than one year and the consequences are likely to last for many years. This means that many aspects other than just how to spend the money, must be brought in.

It will be necessary to plan the timing of the expenditure and the extent of it. More important will be the need to assess whether the project should take place at all or, where there are alternatives competing for the same limited funds, which should be financed and which should be scrapped.

Capital Budget

As with the rest of the budgeting process, this will show the anticipated expenditure of fixed assets for the year but, unlike the other budgets, it does not give an executive order to surge ahead and spend a given sum.

It gives an indication that a sum of money is being put aside for a capital use and the practice is that, when the asset is needed or other purchases are to be made, Capital Requisitions are submitted to top management for approval. With the requisition will come quotations for the supply together with up to date estimates of performance and the expected benefits. Where the budget is in outline, there will need to be a case for the particular purchase.

This will give the top management a chance to review the situation in the light of the pattern that emerges in the year and to make sure the cash resources are available. It could be that with a capital project planned to start near the end of the financial year, a completely different market situation has developed and this may be enough to produce a decision not to proceed. With the long-term implications and often large sums of money involved, care has to be taken that only the profitable projects are undertaken.

Capital Appraisal

Although some of the capital budgets may be planned in outline only, at some stage the project must be appraised.

Several methods are used for this ranging from the simple to those involving sophisticated formulae. Whichever is used there has to be a degree of uncertainty, as once again the future is being examined.

The capital outlay can usually be fixed but the inflow of money resulting from the project is far from certain. For this reason any results must be interpreted with a degree of tolerance. In fact, if the expected profit flow from two assessments which are being appraised were to come to within a few pounds of one another, then some other style of decision-making than financial must be employed.

Pay-back Method

All appraisal circulates around making a choice between alternatives. It may be a choice to buy a new machine or to repair and keep the old one, it could be the choice between two or more different replacements or, looking away from the expenditure aspect, which payment pattern for income should be chosen,

The method which is used by the majority of the companies in the United Kingdom, especially the smaller companies, is the pay-back method. This ranks projects in the order of the speed by which the capital outlay can be recovered by the earnings from the profit. An example in the simplest terms will explain.

There are two machines on the market which will do an identical process equally as efficiently, both are identically priced and each will last five years before going as scrap at a nil value. The net inflow for the machines, that is the revenue less the running expenses, will amount to:

Year	Machine A	Machine B
0	(£5,000)	(£5,000)
1	3,000	1,000
2	3,000	2,000
3	2,000	3,000
4	1,000	3,000
5	1,000	2,000

Using the pay back method for machine A, the outlay of £5,000 will be recovered within a period of one year eight months whereas machine B will make this recovery after two years eight months. On this basis machine A will be chosen as suitable, ignoring the fact that if the overall net receipts are examined machine A has a surplus of £5,000 over the five years while machine B brings in £6,000.

Although this system is easy to use, the failure to examine the overall position is one of the weaknesses. However it does have a place in the sifting of the suitable projects. If payback is used as the primary sorting area, time can be saved. In a more complicated situation, if it can be seen that the project will not be able to payback within, say, twenty years and the asset concerned wears out after ten years, it is senseless to proceed.

Yield method

A further criticism of payback is its complete disregard for the cost of money although it can be argued that one of the expenses incorporated into the net running costs is the cost of borrowing.

To relate a money cost, the yield is produced, that is the percentage of the net proceeds to the outlay, averaged over the life of the project. In the example given for the payback, the effect would be:

Machine A	Surplus (inflow less outflow)		£5,000
	Life		5 years
	Average surplus per year		£1,000
	Average yield	Annual surplus	

$$\frac{\text{Annual surplus}}{\text{Outlay}} = \frac{1000}{5000} = 20\%$$

Machine B	Surplus		£6,000
	Average surplus per year		£1,200
	Average yield	$\dfrac{1200}{5000}$ =	24%

On this basis machine B would be chosen as the investment to make, provided, of course, the yield rate exceeds the average cost of capital for the company.

While this method is better than the payback, in that it does bring in the cost of capital and does look at the overall picture, the use of the discounting technique gives a finer result.

Once again, it can be used in the screening process. If the project shows a yield of one or two percent, when the target yield for the company is in excess of fifteen, there is no need to waste time proceeding.

Discounting techniques

A fault with both the payback and the yield method is the total disregard that they have for the pattern of the inflow and outflow. In the example given both inflows differ, with the peak for machine A being early in the life, while with machine B, it comes near the end of the expected life. This will have an effect on both the recovery of the outlay and the point of use that the company has for the surplus. In addition, there will be an effect on the cost of the borrowing of the money due to the time the sum borrowed will be outstanding.

In effect, with the general methods, there is no comparison of like with like.

The common base used is the present value of the money flows involved. This is for two reasons. With the projects going into the future there is only one time which is certain, today. The second reason is the time value of money.

All money has a time value, if it is freely disposable. In this, it is assumed that the sum paid or received can be invested freely and will obtain a chosen rate of interest.

The question can then be asked, which is it preferable to have, a sum of money received at a given time in the future, or to have the same sum now and be free to invest it? The answer is to have the sum now. The problem is to find the sum needed now which, taking into account compound interest, will produce the future sum.

There exist formulae to do this but for general use tables have been prepared to show factors which, when multiplied by sum to be received or paid a certain number of time periods ahead, will give the present value for each rate of interest.

The tables are so designed that there is no need to worry about currency to be used, provided it is the same for all the calculations and uses the decimal base. The interest is the rate applied per period. This allows the period used to be other than one year, although this is the usual period taken.

Other features which are usually brought in when using the techniques are: the starting point becomes the beginning of the first period, that is, at present; the periodic receipts or payments (other than one which occurs at the beginning) are taken to occur at the end of the period concerned. There is a technique for adjusting for part periods but for this the reader is referred to a specialist text.

It is also possible to counter the effects of expected inflation and the recovery of allowances or the making of payments of tax, on the project.

The best allegory for the discounting technique is to think of compounding in reverse. In compounding the starting point is the present and the interest earned is added at the end of each period to the sum invested and this is re-invested for a given number of periods. Here the starting point is the future time and the sum taken includes the re-invested interest to be removed to find the original sum.

Net present value

The intention will be to reduce each of the future inflows back to the present value and to reduce the sum of these by the outlay. The result will be the net present value of each financial pattern and the higher result will be the more profitable project.

Although this will not occur in the example of machine A versus machine B, should one of the net present value calculations result in a negative quantity, this will mean the inflow is not sufficient to recover the cost plus interest charges at the chosen rate over the period concerned.

Firstly, the appropriate rate of interest must be chosen. It may be the rate at present or the rate considered to be the average cost of capital over the period reviewed.

Secondly, on the table for the Present Value of 1 (reproduced here as table 1 in the appendix) the factor corresponding with the rate of interest and the year of receipt is found and this is multiplied by the inflow. This gives the present value.

Thirdly, the process is repeated for each inflow, all the present values added together and the outlay subtracted. This is repeated to each machine.

The result will appear:

Year	Machine A £ × Factor = PV			Interest rate 8% Machine B £ × Factor = PV		
0	(5,000)		(5,000)	(5,000)		(5,000)
1	3,000	0.926	2,778	1,000	0.926	926
2	3,000	0.857	2,571	2,000	0.857	1,714
3	2,000	0.794	1,588	3,000	0.794	2,382
4	1,000	0.735	735	3,000	0.735	2,205
5	1,000	0.681	681	2,000	0.681	1,362
Net present value			£3,353			3,589

Machine B has the higher positive result and so on financial grounds this is the project to be chosen.

There are times when the flow of cash in a DCF calculation is a series of repetitive amounts and to have to calculate each out individually would be very tedious. This is not necessary as a table has been devised for this (reproduced here as table 2 in the appendix).

To take the previous example with machine A, suppose the inflow instead of being erratic had been a constant £2,000 per year in each of the five years. The factor would have been found in table 2, headed PV of 1 received per period, by taking the last year concerned against the interest rate, this time 8%, as 3.993. This gives a present value (PV) of £7,986 (the factor times the annual amount) and a net present value (NPV) of £2,986.

Should an annuity table not be available the same effect can be obtained by adding the factors from table 1, up to the period concerned and then multiplying. In the example, these would amount to the same, although sometimes there is a slight difference in the last digit due to the rounding process.

Internal Rate of Return (IRR)

At times management is not concerned with whether the project will recover the outlay or with finding which will be the most profitable. They may wish to know the rate of return the project will achieve after the recovery of the outlay.

This has to be done by trial and error. In this example there is a machine costing £4,000 to give the inflow set out in the calculation for each of five years at £1,000; £1,000; £1,200; £1,200; and £900 – a total inflow of £5,300.

Firstly, the approximate rate needed is found. To do this the excess of the inflow over the outlay is taken, £5,300 minus £4,000, to equal £1,300. Divide by the expected life and this will give £260. Express this as the percentage of *half* of the investment, here £260/50%(4,000) = 13%.

The method will be to take a rate near to this and multiply the inflows by the factors for each year until the addition of the present values amounts to £4,000. A rate of interest will be found to give a result above this amount and one below. In this case the rates of 8% and 12% were finally found and the results are given:

Year	Amount	Factor @ 8%	= PV	@ 12%	= PV
1	£1,000	0.926	£ 926	0.893	£ 893
2	1,000	0.857	857	0.797	797
3	1,200	0.794	953	0.712	854
4	1,200	0.735	882	0.636	763
5	900	0.681	613	0.567	510
			4844		3817

This will mean that the rate of return is greater than eight but lower than 12%. The actual rate can be found by using the simple mathematical process of extrapolation. Reduce each by the amount of the outlay and add the two differences together. This gives 1,661. The actual rate will be the proportion of 844 to

191

1,661 of the difference between the rates, that is the 4% plus the original 8%.

In figures $8\% + \dfrac{(4\% \times 844)}{1661} = 8\% + 2.032\%$

$= 10.032\%$ which is the return earned.

Chapter Twenty
Groups of Companies

A feature of modern business is the tendency to form groups of companies. No longer in the structure of business in the Western Hemisphere is it usual to find a single company structure operating through branches and divisions unless the retail trade is involved or the company has only one product.

This has come about for several reasons. As companies expand and diversify they look for other enterprises which can be merged in with their own activity. The shares are purchased in the other company and control is obtained.

If the new business is operating in a satisfactory way, it is then built up on its existing semi-independent structure with control coming through the power of the majority shareholding to appoint directors.

This take-over situation may be the need for rationalization or the elimination of competition. It may be merely for the need to grow bigger.

As an alternative, when a new activity is started, a company can be incorporated to carry this part on. This has a further advantage over the branch structure. Should the new venture fail or even another part of the group of companies get into financial difficulties, then one collapse will not bring down the whole. If there is a serious failure in a branch, the whole enterprise is affected. With separate companies, each, in the eyes of the law, is separate and an independent legal person.

If this company fails, the company owning the shares will suffer no more than losing its investment, while should the owning company fail then the shares forming the investment can be sold off. In the second case, this is not always easy as a willing buyer needs to be found, usually in haste.

What is a Group?

Certain terminology has been introduced. A company that holds a majority of the equity shares in another company or in some other manner controls it is known as the HOLDING COMPANY and in popular terms, the PARENT COMPANY. The company owned is the SUBSIDIARY COMPANY and in some countries these are the daughter companies. When a third tier of companies is introduced, controlled by the subsidiary, this becomes a SUB-SUBSIDIARY and the company at head of the chain will then be the ultimate holding company. All the companies taken together as a collective term are a GROUP OF COMPANIES.

Often there is a structure with the holding company having several subsidiaries and these may or may not have their own subsidiaries. The relationship between these subsidiaries is not direct and, strictly speaking, they have no influence on each other except by a common policy through the top. They are known as FELLOW-SUBSIDIARIES, although recently the name of ASSOCIATED COMPANIES is being used to describe this relationship. This use of the term 'associate' is not strictly correct in the United Kingdom definition, as will be described later.

What is Control?

Under United Kingdom law there is control when more than half of the voting shares are owned by another company. It needs to be only one share over the half for the control to be achieved.

At times this may occur indirectly in the larger groups when a subsidiary takes an interest in another company in which the parent company or a fellow subsidiary is already a shareholder. If the beneficial shareholding is found to be over half, the last company must be brought into the group.

The beneficial shareholding refers to the proportion of voting shares held in another company. For example, if the holding company owns 75% in subsidiary A which in turns holds 60% of the shares in its subsidiary B, the beneficial holding by the parent in B is three-quarters of 60% equal to 45%, which on grounds of share-ownership would not bring company B into the group.

This could be used as a means of evading the law and so additional tests are used. If the parent company controls the composition of the board of directors in another company, then that company becomes a subsidiary. This would bring company B in the example above into the group.

As an alternative, if the parent company is able to control more than half the assets in another company, the parent/subsidiary relationship will again exist.

The Main Implication in Grouping

Excluding the main implication that the parent company has the practical day to day control over the subsidiaries, the law in the United Kingdom imposes some financial duties on the parent company. Under the Companies Acts, each year companies must publish their accounts and this regulation applies to both the private and the public companies alike. The only exception to the strict rule is in the rare occasion where there is an unlimited company.

In addition, the ultimate holding company in the United Kingdom must publish a consolidated profit and loss account together with the balance sheet to include the whole group. Should there be intermediate holding companies, as in the situation where a subsidiary has its own subsidiary, there is no obligation to publish consolidated accounts at that level, although for information and publicity reasons these are often prepared.

The reasoning behind such a requirement is to to allow other companies or persons dealing with the group to see the true position. If the requirement to produce group accounts was not present, it would be possible for unscrupulous owners and directors to fragment their groups to conceal the true position.

Many possibilities could be introduced. Profits could be manipulated to make it appear that a main company was making a loss while another subsidiary took the profits to distribute them for personal gain.

It is only when there are some overseas subsidiaries which would encourage trading difficulties if there was disclosure, or where the activities in the subsidiary are so different the resulting consolidation would be misleading, can exception be made. In these cases, authority needs to be obtained prior to publication from the appropriate government department.

How Consolidation is Achieved

The overall objective is to bring the financial statements of the parent company and all the statements of the parent company and all the subsidiaries together to show the financial position related to the external aspects of the group. What goes on inside, between the various companies does not affect the outsiders and so needs to be ignored in the final presentation of information.

As the profit and loss account (the income statement) is really an analysis of the retained profit figure in the balance sheet (the financial statement) it will be ignored for the purpose of this, other than to state the charges made by one company to another within the group, the inter-group income or the inter-group profits become self-cancelling.

This principle applies throughout the consolidation procedure. What is taken as a charge (an expense or cost) by one company of the group, is cancelled out as it is taken as revenue by another.

When preparing consolidated accounts the inter-group trading is eliminated first and then the inter-group indebtedness. What is a debtor in the records of one company will be found as an equal creditor in the records of another.

For loans and other borrowing, this is a simple operation but there are some difficulties when it comes to the shareholding by the holding company in the subsidiary. Unfortunately it is rare for the investment to be made by the holding company at the same price as the value of the assets taken over. Sometimes there is a premium paid and on other occasions there is a purchase at a price lower than the book value of the assets show. This difference has to be calculated as it must remain after the matching of the investment to the amount taken.

If there is a premium paid, this excess is termed GOOD-WILL and will be shown in the consolidated balance sheet as an intangible asset and the opposite situation is known as there being a CAPITAL RESERVE created. Should there be more than one subsidiary, any goodwill or capital reserve created on consolidation will be set against the other and the net amount shown. Normally, it is the goodwill which is the greater.

A further complication comes in the calculation of the goodwill through the retained profits of the subsidiary. The profits need to be divided into the pre-acquisition profits, those earned prior to the acquisition, and the post-acquisition profits, those earned subsequent to take-over. The pre-acquisition profits are counted as a part of the purchase price paid by the holding company.

The explanation for this is that those profits were earned by the efforts and the investment of the previous owners and it is logical that, if the holding company is buying in, they should pay for the past success and not receive these profits as a gift.

Similar treatment is given to the non-revenue reserves in the subsidiary.

The practical steps taken to calculate the goodwill or capital reserve is to subtract from the cost of the investment in the holding company the value of their acquisition. This is found by percentage of their interest in the subsidiary as applied to the nominal share capital and the reserves of the subsidiary.

For example, if the purchase price were £90,000 and the investment were to take 75,000 shares of £1 each from a nominal capital of £100,000, this would be a 75% interest. If the reserves amounted to £10,000, the holding company would be acquiring 75% of the £100,000 and 75% of the £10,000 or £82,500. As the holding company paid £90,000 for an interest with a book value of £82,500, the premium paid (the goodwill) is £7,500.

When calculating the group profit for the balance sheet, all the profit and the reserves of the parent company are taken plus the proportion of the total post-acquisition profits in each subsidiary, calculated on the basis of the holding company's interest in the nominal capital of each subsidiary. In the example given, this was 75%, so 75% of the post-acquisition profits would be treated as a part of the group profit.

In many acquisitions the percentage interest taken does not reach 100%. When it does the subsidiary becomes a WHOLLY-OWNED SUBSIDIARY. In the example, the interest was 75% and the remaining 25% is held by what is known as the MINORITY INTEREST. Should the subsidiary need to be sold, they are entitled to 25% of any net proceeds, so it is correct for their rights to be recognized.

This could be done by taking the balance sheet of the subsidiary and apportioning all the assets and liabilities between the holding company and the minority shareholders, but this would be misleading. For example, if the main assets of the subsidiary were buildings and other property, to show a value of 75% of the amount appearing in the individual company balance sheet would give the user of the consolidated account a distorted picture.

To overcome this defect, no attempt is made to divide the assets and the liabilities, but they are taken into the consolidated accounts in full and the minority interest shown as a liability by the group. This acknowledges in the event of the assets of the subsidiary being sold the group has a liability to pay the minority a certain sum.

This is calculated by totalling the amount of the interest the minority has in the nominal capital plus a similar proportion of the reserves. In this case there is no need to distinguish between pre- and post-acquisition reserves. They all belong to the minority shareholders as they did not buy in.

Finally, as has been mentioned when examining the position of the minority, assets and liabilities, once the inter-group activity has been removed, appear in the consolidated balance sheet. The amounts shown could be said to be related to the external user.

From a practical point of view, it will be found that when examining consolidated balance sheets, the capital of the group will always be the capital of the parent company. This comes about as the capital of the subsidiary is either eliminated against the investment by the holding company or will be reflected in the minority interest.

Associated Companies

There is very often the situation, whether from choice or otherwise, in which the investing company does not hold more than 50% in the capital of another company, but at the same time does hold an interest substantial enough to be able to put pressure on the directors in their day to day administration. As there is not more than a 50% holding, there is no need to present consolidated accounts and there could arise a situation where a loss or a profit in the investment could be concealed.

In the United Kingdom, a substantial interest is taken to mean more than 20% but not more than 50%. When investments fall into this category the proportion of the profit based on the investment must be brought into the profit and loss account of the investing company. It must be reflected as well in the value of the investment for associated companies in the balance sheet by adding the profits to the original cost.

One major point must be taken into consideration when using the figures for the associated companies. The figure of the profit is taken from the latest set of accounts to be published by the associate. This differs from the accounts of a group where, by law, all the accounting dates of the companies in the group must coincide unless a very good reason can be given to the authorities why it should not. This can arise for overseas subsidiaries when, by the law, in that country, the accounts of all companies, registered in the country, must terminate on a certain day.

The effect will be that, in the case of the associate, the profit being brought in could be related to an accounting period of nearly twelve months earlier.

Disclosure of Holding

The pressure the minority shareholders can apply to the directors in the control of a company has been mentioned in connection with the associate company. Sometimes due to the fragmented nature of the shareholdings this influence can be felt at levels of investment below 20%. For this reason, in the United Kingdom, if a company finds that over 5% of its capital or of any class of shares is concentrated in the hands of one individual or one company, details of the true owner, where these are possible to obtain, must be shown as information in the accounts. If the company, finding this level, is listed on the Stock Exchange, then the stock exchange needs to be told of any changes in those holdings.

This is to show other investors where pressure may be exerted and to be able to foresee any likely takeover bids. The use of United Kingdom nominees to conceal such holdings is not permitted.

Nominees are used when the real holder of the shares or other security does not wish, often for very good and honest reasons, to disclose his ownership to the company and subsequently, through the company having to send a list of all shareholders to the government registry, to any person who cares to examine the records.

Chapter Twenty-one

Mergers and Takeovers

The effects of a successful takeover have been discussed in the last chapter, and this chapter takes the matter further to look at the methods used.

What is a Takeover?

When one company acquires sufficient shares in another to gain control, it is said to have taken over the other. This does not imply that the second company will automatically lose its separate identity, merely its independence. In fact, very often for taxation reasons there is the situation in which the bidding company, although acquiring the other company, will then absorb itself into it and lose its own identity. This is the reverse take-over.

At times two companies will decide to merge their interests and there are two main variations of this. The two companies can continue on their independent ways but all of their shares are held by a third company, formed for the purpose and owned by the former shareholders in the individual companies. Alternatively, all the assets in both the companies can be sold to a new company which will trade under a different title. The shares in the new company are exchanged for the shares in the separate companies in accordance with a pre-arranged formula.

Unless there is a 50–50% holding in the new company, this can be another form of takeover by the dominant partner.

A further form of combination in business is becoming popular, especially in connection with finance and banking or in large scale construction and engineering work. This is the CONSORTIUM COMPANY. In order to carry out a venture too big for the resources of any one member, several companies join together to form a new company in which they all invest in an agreed proportion. No member holds a share of the capital which will cause the holding company/subsidiary arrangement to develop but very often there is the associated company status. Management is provided by the partner companies.

When a partner wishes to leave there is usually a stipulation that the shares must be sold to the remaining members and then it is possible for one investing company to gain a majority position.

In practical terms a consortium has proved to be a very satisfactory way of carrying out a large venture where there is a risk content as, due to there being a separate company formed, the partner companies will only lose their investment in the event of failure and will be able to protect the funds of their own investors. If there are profits their own shareholders gain directly as, in most legislations, it is the owning companies who are taxed and not the consortium. This has a marked effect on how losses and reliefs against profit are dealt with.

Why are Mergers Necessary?

Most of the reasons are the same in practice as those found in an economics textbook. There is the desire to eliminate competition by taking over the rival.

This appears in another form when attempts are made to rationalize the structure of a particular industry and, either with the inducement of the government or from choice, several companies join together to form a larger unit which, in theory, will be able to attain a stronger market position than if they operated independently. There is the need for vertical integration, either to ensure sources of supply or to give better sales outlets. Sometimes this is done in part only to secure supplies of a vital component or even to stop a supplier, who has financial troubles, from going into liquidation.

Diversification of interests is often put forward as another reason and in the 1950s and 1960s huge groups of companies were formed. These were known as conglomerates. While they were able to spread the investment risks and, at first, earn good profits due to their size, they have lost a great deal of their attraction, not from lack of finance but from the inability to find suitable management able to control such diverse activities.

Finally, there remains an unfortunate reason for takeover of another company. That is the need for extra power. Sometimes these are successful and the only reason they exist at all is the whim of one person or of a group.

Methods used in Takeovers

Several methods can be used and the most popular for the smaller companies comes with negotiation. This will also be found often in the merger situation.

For companies with shares listed on the stock exchanges, the initial stages are usually different. The bidding company will buy as many shares as it can on the open market without pushing the price beyond a target amount or without triggering a holding level which forces it to make an immediate bid for all the other shares it does not hold.

Its tactics in this are usually decided in consultation with its financial advisors, and the merchant banks make a speciality of this service. Once it is seen that a takeover bid may be coming the 'victim' company also calls in its advisors, either to prepare a defence or to start negotiations for a settlement.

The price for the bid is fixed and if the directors of the target company do not agree that it is sufficient, details will then be sent to all the shareholders. It is this part which distinguishes the bids made in the United Kingdom from those made in many other countries. By custom and government encouragement most shares are registered and the names of the holders appear on the register of members together with the addresses (used to send out the dividends, so they are normally up-to-date). The few bearer shares in existence must be placed with an authorised depository, usually a bank or a lawyer. This is a requirement of the exchange control laws.

There is a contrast here with some other countries where the majority of the shares and other securities are in bearer form, with the result it is almost impossible to approach the shareholders other than through the press and other media. This probably accounts for the lack of contested takeovers in many countries.

The bid is made to the shareholders who decide whether to accept or not at that price, or whether to wait to accept at a revised price. Their acceptance is conditional on the bidding company's being able to reach a certain percentage of acceptances. When this percentage is reached the announcement is made and the bid is unconditional. This has to be made within a given time or the offers lapse.

At this stage the battle is almost over.

Sometimes there is a counterbid by another company and when the matter is finally settled the unsuccessful bidder is left holding those shares it had purchased on the open market in the early stages. This may or may not be to its advantage for although it has not achieved the main objective it may sell the shares at a later time and make a very substantial profit.

If the bidding company obtains a holding in the subsidiary of 90% or over, it can force the holders of the remaining shares to sell to them at a fair price.

The Practical Implications

Once the takeover is complete, the buying company has several ways in which to deal with the company it has acquired. It can leave it trading under its own name, although it is most likely there will be a substantial change in the membership of the board of directors.

As an alternative it can transfer the assets to itself or to another company in the group and then either liquidate the subsidiary or hold it as a 'shell' company to preserve its name and possibly some trade marks.

In practice the procedure is to sell the assets to another company and from the proceeds to distribute these to the parent company, but this has to be done carefully to preserve taxation status.

A third method would be to merge with another company or for both companies to merge into a third company. Once again this needs very careful thought and professional advice due to the tax position. In the United Kingdom, a company trading before the introduction of Corporation Tax in 1965 paid its tax on 1 January in the year of the assessment based on the profits shown in the accounts of the company's financial year previous. If the company year ended on 30 April, 1964 it would pay its taxes for 1965/66, which are based on the profits of that year, on 1 January 1966. This gave a use of government money, free of interest for twenty months.

After 1965 they were allowed to pay at the same date as they would have done if Corporation Tax had not been introduced but new companies or companies which had changed their status (such as a holding company) paid nine months after the end of their financial year.

If the company being taken over pays its tax under the old scheme but the parent company pays after nine months, there is a case for arranging the takeover in such a manner. The parent company reverses back into the subsidiary, with the roles becoming reversed, and a very useful tax bonus becomes available.

Controls on Takeovers

If takeovers were allowed to proceed without control a situation could arise in a country to harm its economy. Instead certain curbs have had to be introduced in most countries, if only to ensure that control of the country does not get into the wrong hands.

In the United Kingdom, the conduct of the companies involved and their advisors is monitored through a voluntary code of practice. These are the so-called TAKEOVER RULES and the guiding body is the CITY PANEL FOR TAKEOVERS AND MERGERS. This body is appointed by the Stock Exchange and certain other financial interests. Its powers are very wide and to break the rules invokes sanctions in the financial centre at London.

Should the proposed merger not be in the national interest or put the companies concerned in a monopoly position in the market, the Office of Fair Trading will intervene by referring the matter for consideration by the Monopolies Commission.

They may give a legally enforceable order that the merger cannot go through.

If the takeover is from overseas, the Bank of England has the power to block the completion by refusing to allow the funds necessary to be invested in this country.

Other countries have similar bodies able to control takeovers.

Chapter Twenty-two

Liquidations, Reconstructions and Valuations

When a company gets into financial difficulties it has three courses of action open to it. It can liquidate and distribute its assets to pay off the creditors, it can enter into an agreement with its creditors for a future plan of payment or it can reconstruct, continue to trade and compensate the creditors in various ways.

Liquidation

At times a company has no choice but to be put into liquidation. This can happen when a creditor is not prepared to wait any longer for settlement of a debt and obtains an order from the Court for payment. If the order is not obeyed and if it is above a certain amount, winding-up procedures can be started. This form of winding-up is a COMPULSORY WINDING-UP under the control of the Court.

If the company realizes its predicament, before there is a petition for winding-up presented to the Court, the directors can call a meeting of the shareholders and agree to liquidate the company. Should the company not be able to pay all its debts, this becomes a CREDITORS' WINDING-UP. If the debts can be paid and the reason for winding-up is not due to the liabilities exceeding the asset value, then the winding-up is termed a MEMBERS' WINDING-UP, with the associated legal procedures not as onerous as in the other methods.

Whichever method is used, the procedure is similar. As soon as the winding-up begins, the powers of the directors cease and pass to the LIQUIDATOR. This aptly named official is usually an accountant, who takes over the company, sells off the assets and as far as the proceeds allow, pays off the creditors in the order of the priority they have. Any money left over goes to repaying the shareholders and a surplus remaining is shared out between the ordinary shareholders – the holders of the equity in the company.

Unfortunately most liquidations are carried out as the company cannot pay its debts and it is the holders of the secured debts who manage to get a part repayment leaving nothing for the unsecured creditors or the shareholders. In really bad cases it is only debts which have a legal priority to payment, such as to the revenue authorities, who are satisfied, leaving the rest with a valueless security.

Arrangement

Sometimes it is felt that a liquidation is too drastic a remedy. It could be that, if the company were to go into liquidation, the unsecured creditors would receive nothing or very little but if the company were to be helped over a difficult period, it could return to profitable trading in the very near future.

In these circumstances an ARRANGEMENT is made with *all* the creditors for a compromise solution. Two courses are usually followed. The creditors may agree to receive only a proportion of their debt in final settlement or the secured creditors agreed to subordinate their claims until the unsecured have been paid, in other words they forego their priority.

An alternative is for a MORATORIUM to be considered. The creditors agree to wait for a period of time, say one year, before they will get their payments and then it may be a payment by instalments. Such arrangements need to be notified to the appropriate government department so that all persons likely to deal with the company can see that the arrangement is in existence.

Reconstruction

Even with a scheme of arrangement, the structure of the company could be so distorted by the events that have occurred, that it can no longer reflect through a balance sheet a true and fair view of its state. The capital may be lost, the assets grossly overstated, or it may be a combination of both.

When this occurs the company can revalue its assets and then ask the Court for authority for a REDUCTION OF CAPITAL. If the Court considers, after this has been done, that the company will be able to trade in a better and more realistic form, they will agree. Sometimes where there is surplus capital, not a loss, they will agree to a part of the value of the shares being repaid to the shareholders. This usually happens after a takeover and the subsidiary changes its trading pattern.

To protect creditors who deal with the company subsequently the Court may order the words 'and reduced' to be added to the name for a specified period.

On occasions a re-modelling of the capital structure of the company will not be sufficient and it may be that the best course of action to RECONSTRUCT the company completely by forming a new company and selling all the assets from the old to it.

Several advantages can arise from this. The assets can be brought into the new at a realistic value and assets which have been lost can be ignored. Old debts can be wiped out for, if the arrangements can be made with the creditors of the old company, they may be persuaded to exchange their unsecured debt for a secured form or even shares in the new company. With existing security holders the terms can be altered in respect of the rate of interest to be paid or to the dates of repayment.

Valuation

When the creditors are trying to assess which of the courses they should take, it is very likely they should wish to value the company.

If it is a public company with the shares quoted on the stock exchange, this is very easy. The share price gives the market assessment of value and by multiplying this amount by the number of shares on issues a value can be obtained.

The problems can occur when the company is not quoted and four main methods of valuation are in general use – book value, replacement value, break-up value, and the going concern value which may be the market value.

Book value

Of these, the book value is the easiest to find but is the least indicative of the value. It is found by taking the net capital employed – the fixed and current assets less the current liabilities. Whether or not the long-term liabilities or such items as the preference shares are also subtracted will depend on the use it is intended to apply.

Replacement value

This is found from catalogues and other current price lists. It is the value of the assets needed to restart the business from new at the present time.

Break-up value

The break-up value reflects the amounts expected to be realized in the event of a liquidation. Some of the assets, such as property might exceed the book value by a substantial margin but most of the others are likely to be well below. This fall in value will be most apparent in the stock.

The figure showing in the books is the cost and the value the company will incorporate into the costing and possibly the pricing systems. It is effectively the value in use. If the stock is sold under other circumstances a large fall in value can be expected, unless the stock is a rare commodity, such as a precious metal.

Two factors govern this fall. First, the company exists to sell the stock as finished goods. If it is selling to other users it is not structured for this and is likely to find severe restriction in the number of outlets. Secondly, if it unloads a large quantity on to a market already full from the sales by the usual suppliers, a glut is possible and the surplus from an unusual source will suffer the full effects of the economics law of supply and demand, with the price falling out.

A final factor depressing the price, and possibly meaning that the sale will have to be to a scrap merchant or a merchant specializing in bankrupt stock, will be that the quantity put onto the market for each item will be too small for the usual order size.

All these combining will mean the value to be realized will be between 10% and 25% of the book value.

Going concern value

If these three methods of valuation are not suitable, it may be better to value the company as a going concern.

In the listed company this is done by taking the market price of the shares. This can only happen in the other companies if there has been an official valuation, such as for the calculation of death duties, within a reasonable period before. Alternatively the services of professional valuers can be used and they will compare the value of the company with that of a similar company, with which they are familiar and have recently valued or sold.

For general purposes, it is possible to assess a going-concern or market value by using a similar technique, comparing the value of the company with an existing corporation.

To do this a similar company is chosen where the shares are quoted on a stock exchange and from the statistical information presented the price/earnings ratio (P/E ratio) is found. How this can be calculated is set out in the next chapter.

This ratio gives the market assessment of the worth of the company and, in technical terms, does this by discounting a flow of future earnings rate as an indicator as to how quickly the investment can be recovered.

In the company to be valued the earnings rate is calculated for each share and the result multiplied by the P/E ratio of the chosen company. This produces the 'market' price for each share and to find the capitalization value of the company, it is only necessary to multiply by the number of ordinary shares on issue.

This method is somewhat similar to the 'number of years' profit purchased' method used when selling a partnership.

Chapter Twenty-three

Assessing the Investments

In earlier chapters the use of control ratios was discussed. These were for liquidity, performance and structure but there was one area omitted – investment.

Just as there needs to be an appraisal before an investment is made, there must be a control process afterwards. This is done through ratios.

Return on Investment

When dealing with an operational project, it is easy to take the sum invested and to relate the profit attributable to it, to give the return on investment. When the investment is through shares this process is not so easy as the choice of the investment base plays an important part.

A simple ratio could be the share ratio. This is the ratio of the profit to the nominal value of the shares but it would not be indicative of progress. In many countries the structure of the capital is to have a very small nominal capital from shares, whether these are of the ordinary variety or having a degree of preference or priority. With the modern tendency to retain as reserve the nominal share capital bears no real relationship to the shareholders' interests.

The share issue price, where this was at a premium, could be used but once again the fact that the reserves created from operating are omitted prevents any real measurement of the performance of the investment.

When the revenue reserves are added as well, the effect is the return on the net worth and if the preference share capital is omitted, the return on equity can be found. In this case it is usual to take the profit as the amount due to the equity holders, that is, after interest, preference dividends and taxation.

The main disadvantage of the equity figure is that it is purely a book amount and does not reflect the return on the investment made by the individual shareholder who purchases his shares in the market.

The Dividend Yield

The investor is generally interested in the amount due to him, not to other shareholders, and so any return calculated must be related to the market price of the share. If the shareholder is measuring the present return it will be the market price at the date of purchase but if the figure is needed for changing investments, it will be the current price on the day.

For many years the return to the shareholder was based not on the profits of the company but on the dividend the company pay out and the DIVIDEND YIELD is found by:

$$\frac{\text{Current dividend per share}}{\text{Market price per share}} \times 100$$

To avoid the distortions caused by some taxation systems deducting income tax at source, the gross figure before tax is normally taken when the ratio is needed for comparison purposes.

A disadvantage in using the dividend yield as a measure of the performance of a share has been the change in dividend policies since the 1950s.

With the high cost of money, high taxation, and, sometimes, government restrictions on the amount which can be declared, companies have tended to stabilize their dividends at a low figure and to reinvest the rest of the profits back into the business. The result is to destroy the dividend yield as a satisfactory measuring device except for looking at personal income.

In spite of this disadvantage, many popular newspapers give this yield along with the closing share prices in their share listings. The newspapers catering more for the financial sectors of the community will usually add further ratios relating to earnings.

Earnings Yield

When profits are retained, the investor may not have the money in his pocket to spend at the time but it is not lost forever. Should the company terminate trading and the assets sold, the equity holders will recover any remaining retentions at that time. This means that their share has risen in value, according to the books, from being merely the nominal value to the nominal share value plus a proportion of the reinvested profit.

As the company is not expected to terminate but to continue as a going concern, the share market recognizes this and reflects the reinvestment in the price. The price of the share will rise to a level including, amongst other factors, the extra proportion expected.

For this reason the amount earned by the company having the use of the funds concerned is far more important than just the dividend of the retained profit. The first comes out in the cash, the second through the price, but the earnings show the overall performance and can ignore the artificial dividend policies which have been brought about.

To find the EARNINGS PER SHARE is, in its simplest form, a matter of dividing the earnings by the number of ordinary shares.

In practice this is not as easy as it appears due to whether or not the figure should be diluted by (taken to include) any options available on share, such as those coming from convertible debentures. On the other hand, it could be a matter of judgement to decide what are the earnings.

The United Kingdom accountancy profession has attempted to overcome this by the issue of a Statement of Standard Accountancy Practice on the matter.

Once the earnings per share (the EPS) has been calculated it is a simple matter to find the yield:

$$\frac{\text{Earnings per share (after tax)}}{\text{Market price per share}} \times 100 = \text{Earnings yield}$$

Price/Earnings ratio

While the earnings yield ratio produces a figure for the earnings power of all the funds employed in the company for the previous year, being a percentage it is felt to have only limited use. It would be more satisfactory to construct instead an index, which instead of looking at the return on a particular share, can act as a means of comparing the opinion of the market of one share against another. This is done through the PRICE/EARNINGS RATIO which is the reciprocal of the earnings yield:

$$\frac{\text{Market Price per share}}{\text{Earnings per share}}$$

In crude terms it shows how many years it will take, if earnings are maintained at the same level, to recover the investment from earnings. In slightly more technical terms, it shows the market opinion of the strength of the share compared with others, taking into consideration that the price will reflect a discounted flow of future earnings at the same level for ever.

The higher the ratio, the safer the share is considered to be, the lower, the greater the risk and to compensate for this the higher the earnings are expected to go.

In practice, as always, a simple interpretation of the index is difficult. It could be that the share is said to be staid with low steady earnings on a high asset value backing for the share (the high asset backing will cause the share price to be high). On the other hand, a low P/E ratio does not mean that the company is on the brink of disaster.

For the reason of the various factors which go to make up the price of a share it is difficult to use the ratio as an indicator across the whole width of the market in shares. It is better to divide it up into sectors, as the market is itself normally divided up, that is comparing all shipping shares or all banking shares. Then it will be either the mean (the average) or the median point (the middle point) in each chosen sector which can be used as the reference point.

Dividend and Interest Cover

Two other investment ratios are in general use. The first is the INTEREST COVER.

Interest must be paid whether there are earnings or not and the holders of debentures and other long term loans will wish to see the safety margin. Shareholders will be interested in this, as well, for the greater the number of times the earnings can cover the interest, the more is left for them. To calculate the figure:

$$\frac{\text{Earnings in accounting period}}{\text{Interest payable in period}} = \text{times covered}$$

The shareholders, to monitor their safety, will find just to bring in the interest, is not enough. Two other items must be covered for them.

The first is the dividend due to the preference shareholders, which is fixed in amount and must be met before they can obtain any dividend on their shares. The second is the rental charges payable for leased equipment.

Failure to pay this is just as serious as failure to pay interest on secured loans. With a loan, failure brings in the receiver to take over the business, while failure to pay the rental will lead to repossession of the equipment and, depending on the extent of the leasing, either a cessation of production or a severe cutback. Either way, the earnings for the shareholders will come down.

Finally a prudent business will not wish to distribute all its earnings as dividend. It will wish to save some, to retain it for adverse times or to retain it for the future advantage of the shareholders. To see the measure of this policy the DIVIDEND COVER is calculated, simply by dividing the earnings after the payment of tax, interest, rental charges and preference dividends by the dividend on the ordinary shares for the period.

Chapter Twenty-four

Audits

All manner of systems can be introduced and subsequent routines can control these and monitor the results but if the checking is built in, it could be wrong in the first place and have an inherent weakness. In addition, through a weakness in the system, it may be possible for an employee to exploit this for his own advantage or gain.

There is a need for an independent check and at this stage in the development of technology this will be, at least partially, by humans.

Two forms are used by most companies. The compulsory audit carried out by external accountants appointed for the purpose, and an internal scheme using employees. The internal audit will not be found in the smaller firms as a separate function although its use can bring considerable savings in overall costs.

External Audit

In the United Kingdom all limited liability companies must appoint auditors whose task it is to make sure the published accounts of the business in the current year.

They are firms of accountants whose partners belong to one of the accountancy professional associations approved by the government for the purpose.

Officially they are appointed by the shareholders each year at the annual general meeting and hold office until the end of the following annual general meeting, with the meeting fixing their remuneration for carrying out their duties. In practice it is effectively the directors who make the appointment.

The firms are independent but there is a weakness in the

system to the extent that the auditors usually act as consultant accountants and taxation advisors to the company as well. While this does ensure that the auditors are able to be involved in the accounting process, there is a risk of a conflict of interest. Sometimes this is made more obvious where the small firm has only one or two main but lucrative audits and, rather than lose these, can be swayed by the directors to overlook items which otherwise should be investigated or amended.

Their job is not that of the police. They are not detectives and should not try to be. If they find fraud or mispractice, they must report this to the directors. If the directors ask them subsequently to investigate further this is a separate issue and away from the appointment of auditor.

They must satisfy themselves that the accounts produced reflect the situation shown in the books and check on the assets, as far as is practicable, to see if they are still in the possession of the company.

Except with the very small company, these days they do not laboriously check every single invoice and transaction but use a sample testing system. This takes a selected block of transactions and follows them through the whole process within the company.

A further task is to make sure all matters required by law to be disclosed in the accounts are disclosed, as well as seeing that, for the quoted company, any additional requirements of Stock Exchange or equivalent security control bodies are included. Now there is an additional duty – making sure the company has prepared the accounts to comply with the many accountancy standards and if they have not done so, to persuade the company concerned to fall into line.

When they are satisfied they must give a certificate to that effect or draw particular attention to any points they do not agree with. This certificate is addressed to the shareholders and a copy must appear with each set of accounts published.

Once, a qualified report, as it is called when the certificate is not clean, was considered a disaster but with the standards produced still in dispute by managements in some sectors of business, these are not uncommon, if only used to protect the auditors.

Internal Audit

This service to management acts as a complement to the external audit. Its main purpose is to ensure the laid down systems are followed and usually there is an additional role with the internal auditors as internal consultants, examining the systems and recommending improvements.

Their duties are not confined to the examination of financial results but go deeper to ensure the policies laid down by the board of directors is not only understood but also being put into action.

Much of their work will be in detail, for example, taking spot checks on the stocks regularly, checking them against the records, and selectively tracing through an issue back to its use on an order from a customer and forward to the recording of the work done through to the sending of the invoice.

This is the part that can save fees being paid to the external auditors who, if they can be satisfied that there is a reliable internal check in operation, will be able to spend their time more effectively.

It is in the efficiency audit where the largest expense saving will come. A good internal audit system will be able to cover the whole of the company and with this overall view will soon be able to see weaknesses and the implication of corrective action which is taken in one sector only.

To perform their task efficiently they will need independence. To make them report to the financial controller or the works director can destroy their effectiveness as conflict of personal interests may arise when criticism of a procedure is necessary.

In these circumstances, the internal audit should report either to the managing director directly or to the group directorate.

Chapter twenty-five

What the Future May Hold

The financial function of a business is not the dead area it has the reputation of being. No longer does it confine its activities to recording what has happened, it has adapted to supplying information for the planning of the future. As new thinking emerges, this is embraced and the new technology is applied to produce extra facts with greater accuracy, in more detail and promptly.

There are six main areas currently being developed:

The use of computers and related technology
Human asset accounting
Social accounting
The adjustment for inflation
Greater disclosure
A move towards the world wide harmonization of the reporting.

Computers

It is probably in the area of financial data processing where there has been the greatest observable impact. In the last four decades has come the change from the use of manual systems with vast armies of clerks recording detail, to the use of a hand-held piece of electronic equipment which can carry out the calculations for the building of financial models to show the future expectations in a split second.

The computers have progressed from a vast complex of valves, connections and rooms full of featureless cupboards, all isolated from the dust-ridden world around them, to a compact desk sized unit which can be operated by semi-skilled labour.

It can be used to record what has happened, to prepare the accounting records and, as a by-product, can be programmed to analyse the information to a depth far greater than was possible or economic under a manual system. Using the latest systems it is possible to recall from the memory banks the state of an account and then to make further entries, run checks and make any necessary corrections before returning the up-dated information to the system for the analysing and allocating it has been programmed to do.

However the greatest advance is not as a speeded up and more accurate accounting machine but in the ability to carry out the calculation for what is termed financial modelling.

The past cannot be changed but to plan for the future the management will need to calculate the possible outcome of their schemes. This often involves a huge number of calculations as all the implications are introduced and then, if there is an undesirable effect, a revised scheme has to be tried.

By using the computer to carry out these calculations, in a very short time the various schemes can be tried and on the basis of the information produced, some costly errors can be avoided.

What is important to remember is that a computer can only be as good as the system for which it has been programmed and as the information which is fed in. Feed in incorrect data at one end and only rubbish can be produced at the other. This only goes to highlight the basic fact – the accounting systems are for information only, they cannot think for themselves and until the human brain is reproduced in an electronic or other form, decisions must come from beyond machines. The human will still be needed to interpret and, it is hoped, to act.

It seems that the next progression will be to use the microprocessors to reduce the size of the equipment even further and also to reduce the unit cost so that even the smallest business will be able to afford a system. With this there will have to come some variation of the bookkeeping method which has survived the last five hundred years almost unscathed.

Human Asset Accounting

In a business there is more than a collection of assets brought together. To put them into action they need humans but up until now this aspect has tended to be ignored.

221

There are three main areas being developed for use. The first is the realization of the effect on staff behaviour of the imposition of financial systems together with the loss or gain in efficiency resulting from this. When turned into financial terms it can have a substantial effect on the final profit figure.

Secondly, there is the recognition of the contribution the employees make to the success of the organization in terms of profit contribution. This is shown in the added value statements which are beginning to be published with the annual report by some companies in the United Kingdom.

In outline this statement shows how the revenue of the company is shared. So much to the cost of purchasing the materials and the operating expenses, the share taken by the employees as wages and salaries, how much goes to the revenue authorities as tax, the amount paid to the shareholders and other investors for the use of their money and finally how much has been left as funds to be re-invested in the business.

In the statements published to date, it seems that the emphasis is to show the proportion being paid to employees.

The third area of interest is to attempt to put a price on the employees. The theory is built up that in a business a known sum of money is spent on machinery which is expected to last for a number of years. The outlay is a capital expense to be recovered over several years against future revenues.

On the other hand, the staff and employee cost is written off in the year in which it is incurred.

For current wages this is reasonable as it represents the hiring to do the job. But what of the cost of hiring, the cost of training and possibly the cost of equipping. Should this be an expense of the year in which it was incurred?

The answer is in doubt as the benefit of the initial expense will be used in the company for many years to come. For this reason these costs should be treated as capital costs and should the employee leave before they have been amortized in full, then the balance will be written off to profit and loss in the same manner as a fixed asset disposed of through obsolesence is treated.

At the moment this concept is still in its infancy.

Social Responsibility Accounting

For centuries many businesses have been carrying on their function with complete disregard to the damage being caused to the environment surrounding them. The fumes from their chimneys may have been destroying the life of those unfortunate enough to live nearby and shortening the life of their employees.

Rightly, some checks have had to be imposed. Various legislations try to protect the health of the employee whilst others attempt to stop toxic waste being dumped freely into rivers and onto the land.

So far this has been done in a physical sense with no direct link to the financial aspects.

Social accounting takes up the activities of the business and attempts to put a figure to the cost of operating a business in its location. The cost of the roads and other facilities needed, the cost of the workers' housing, schools and social services. Then from the company comes an estimate of the damage it is doing to the environment and finally details of the expenditure incurred in trying to minimize the effects.

It is the intention to publish this information with the annual report. In some countries, these reports are compulsory now but only in a very outline form. Whether they will come to be of general application will depend the ability to put a meaningful price to the damage caused or to the measures taken to overcome it.

Inflation Accounting

By far the most controversial matter being developed at the present time is inflation accounting.

Although there are many suggested solutions to the problem, each considered by its sponsors to be the complete answer, the fact of the need to adjust the accounts in some manner is not in doubt.

When a set of accounts is drawn up using the asset values at the time the assets were purchased, there can be a severe distortion. Like cannot be compared with like.

For example, the return on the total assets compares assets valued at their original cost, which could even be fifty years ago, against revenues earned within the last year. Over fifty years 'the purchasing power of money has fallen so dramatically, the meaning of the ratio is no longer indicative of performance.

The whole situation is complicated further by the arrival of what can be called hyper-inflation where there is a substantial rise in the rate of inflation in the accounting period under review. Inflation in excess of twenty percent in a year is no longer the exception and in certain countries the rate over relatively short periods rises in excess of one hundred percent. With this situation there is a need to adjust some of the figures so that an assessment of the position can be made.

The problem is how this should be done.

One attempt is to revalue the assets each year to reflect the replacement value; another uses an index and applies it to all items in the financial statement including the capital and the long term liabilities. Bringing up the asset values to reflect the current purchasing power has been advocated as well as finding the current cost or the current value of the assets. The latest proposal is to find the present value in use to the business but for the moment this is considered to be beyond the practical capabilities.

One thing all these methods have in common is the need to bring the past figure up to the present day values and not to go the other way. The reason is obvious, otherwise the user of the accounts would have the greatest difficulty in relating the results to reality.

A further problem remaining is whether only accounts which have been adjusted for inflation should be published or whether it would be better to publish the accounts on a historical cost basis (at the original cost in most cases) and to show the inflation adjusted results as a set of supplementary sheets.

Finally comes the problem of, having decided on whether to have the two sets of accounts and then which type of adjustment to use, how are the updating statistics and indices to be produced and who will construct them? In many cases there has been a need to fall back on government produced figures as only these are able to be accepted by the greater part of the business community.

Disclosure

Last on the list of the current trends is the growing demand for more and more financial information disclosure. As companies group together to form larger units the shareholders, whether private or institutional, are becoming more and more remote from the management. They wish to know what is happening and the only way they can find this out is from published information.

This is no longer a voluntary task as in many countries legislation is being devised to set out in detail the information needed. The multi-national and international companies will need to disclose the source of their profits in more detail, segmental accounting will be brought in (this is the disclosure of the profit contribution in the various sectors of a company) and much more non-financial detail will be needed as well.

All this will cost money to produce and, to cope with the extraction of the information, systems will have to be designed specifically. There will be benefits as the directors will no longer find it so easy to hide away their inefficiencies or adjust the results to conceal transactions made for tax or exchange control avoidance. Properly used, the need for the extra information could make companies more conscious of the needs of their shareholders.

Linked with disclosure is the international movement for harmonization in the presentation of the financial information. At present each country has its own rules as to how specific items within the published results should be calculated, with the result that it is very difficult to take a set of final accounts from a company in one country and compare it with a set originating in another country.

Already International Standards of Practice are being drawn up and accepted for use by the major industrial and commercial countries. Several are in operation and many more will be published soon.

At a different level, the economic groupings, such as the

European Economic Community, are setting out to harmonize the accounting practices of their member countries and over the next twenty-five years this will have an ever increasing effect.

Even Further Ahead

Beyond the immediate future, what is there to look forward to? What is only at the 'drawing board' stage at present?

Probably the most significant development is Cash Flow Accounting. As has been said many times, the past cannot be changed and does not really give a reliable guide to the future. If future expectations of a company could be projected in such a way as not to reveal commercial secrets but at the same time be expressed in the money terms of today, this would give a real indication of the worth of the company, especially for the creditors and potential shareholders.

And beyond? Who knows...?

Appendix

Appendix

Table A

Present value of £1 to be received n periods hence, interest rate r per period. $v^n = (1+r)^{-n}$

n \ r	2%	4%	6%	8%	10%	12%	14%	16%	18%	20%	22%	24%	26%	28%	30%
1	0·980	0·962	0·943	0·926	0·909	0·893	0·877	0·862	0·847	0·833	0·820	0·806	0·794	0·781	0·769
2	0·961	0·925	0·890	0·857	0·826	0·797	0·769	0·743	0·718	0·694	0·672	0·650	0·630	0·610	0·592
3	0·942	0·889	0·840	0·794	0·751	0·712	0·675	0·641	0·609	0·579	0·551	0·524	0·500	0·477	0·455
4	0·924	0·855	0·792	0·735	0·683	0·636	0·592	0·552	0·518	0·482	0·451	0·423	0·397	0·353	0·350
5	0·906	0·822	0·747	0·681	0·621	0·567	0·519	0·476	0·437	0·402	0·370	0·341	0·315	0·291	0·269
6	0·888	0·790	0·705	0·630	0·564	0·507	0·456	0·410	0·370	0·335	0·303	0·275	0·250	0·227	0·207
7	0·871	0·760	0·665	0·584	0·513	0·452	0·400	0·354	0·314	0·279	0·249	0·222	0·198	0·178	0·159
8	0·853	0·731	0·627	0·540	0·467	0·404	0·351	0·305	0·266	0·233	0·204	0·179	0·157	0·139	0·123
9	0·837	0·703	0·592	0·500	0·424	0·361	0·308	0·263	0·225	0·194	0·167	0·144	0·125	0·108	0·094
10	0·820	0·676	0·558	0·463	0·386	0·322	0·270	0·227	0·191	0·162	0·137	0·116	0·099	0·085	0·073
11	0·804	0·650	0·527	0·429	0·350	0·287	0·237	0·195	0·162	0·135	0·112	0·094	0·079	0·066	0·056
12	0·788	0·625	0·497	0·397	0·319	0·257	0·208	0·168	0·137	0·112	0·092	0·076	0·062	0·052	0·043
13	0·773	0·601	0·469	0·368	0·290	0·229	0·182	0·145	0·116	0·093	0·075	0·061	0·050	0·040	0·033
14	0·758	0·577	0·442	0·340	0·263	0·205	0·160	0·125	0·099	0·078	0·062	0·049	0·039	0·032	0·025
15	0·743	0·555	0·417	0·315	0·240	0·183	0·140	0·108	0·084	0·065	0·051	0·040	0·031	0·025	0·020
16	0·728	0·534	0·394	0·292	0·218	0·163	0·123	0·093	0·071	0·054	0·042	0·032	0·025	0·019	0·015
17	0·714	0·513	0·371	0·270	0·198	0·146	0·108	0·080	0·060	0·045	0·034	0·026	0·020	0·015	0·013
18	0·700	0·494	0·350	0·250	0·180	0·130	0·095	0·069	0·051	0·038	0·028	0·021	0·016	0·012	0·009
19	0·686	0·475	0·331	0·232	0·164	0·116	0·083	0·060	0·043	0·031	0·023	0·017	0·012	0·009	0·007
20	0·673	0·456	0·312	0·215	0·149	0·104	0·073	0·051	0·037	0·026	0·019	0·014	0·010	0·007	0·005
21	0·660	0·439	0·294	0·199	0·135	0·093	0·064	0·044	0·031	0·022	0·015	0·011	0·008	0·006	0·004
22	0·647	0·422	0·278	0·184	0·123	0·083	0·056	0·038	0·026	0·018	0·013	0·009	0·006	0·004	0·003
23	0·634	0·406	0·262	0·170	0·112	0·074	0·049	0·033	0·022	0·015	0·010	0·007	0·005	0·003	0·002
24	0·622	0·390	0·247	0·158	0·102	0·066	0·043	0·028	0·019	0·013	0·008	0·006	0·004	0·003	0·002
25	0·610	0·375	0·233	0·146	0·092	0·059	0·038	0·024	0·016	0·010	0·007	0·005	0·003	0·002	0·001
30	0·552	0·308	0·174	0·099	0·057	0·033	0·020	0·012	0·007	0·004	0·003	0·002	0·001	0·001	*
35	0·500	0·253	0·130	0·068	0·036	0·019	0·010	0·006	0·003	0·002	0·001	0·001	*	*	*
40	0·453	0·208	0·097	0·046	0·022	0·011	0·005	0·003	0·001	0·001	*	*	*	*	*
45	0·410	0·171	0·073	0·031	0·014	0·006	0·003	0·001	0·001	*	*	*	*	*	*
50	0·372	0·141	0·054	0·021	0·009	0·003	0·001	0·001	*	*	*	*	*	*	*

* Less than 0·001.

228

le B

Present value of an annuity of £1 for n periods, interest rate r per period. $a_n = \dfrac{1-(1+r)^{-n}}{r}$

2%	4%	6%	8%	10%	12%	14%	16%	18%	20%	22%	24%	26%	28%	30%
0·980	0·962	0·943	0·926	0·909	0·893	0·877	0·862	0·847	0·833	0·820	0·806	0·794	0·781	0·769
1·942	1·886	1·833	1·783	1·736	1·690	1·647	1·605	1·566	1·528	1·492	1·457	1·424	1·392	1·361
2·884	2·775	2·673	2·577	2·487	2·402	2·322	2·246	2·174	2·106	2·042	1·981	1·923	1·868	1·816
3·808	3·630	3·465	3·312	3·170	3·037	2·914	2·798	2·690	2·589	2·494	2·404	2·320	2·241	2·166
4·713	4·452	4·212	3·993	3·791	3·605	3·433	3·274	3·127	2·991	2·864	2·745	2·635	2·532	2·436
5·601	5·242	4·917	4·623	4·355	4·111	3·889	3·685	3·498	3·326	3·167	3·020	2·885	2·759	2·643
6·472	6·002	5·582	5·206	4·868	4·564	4·288	4·039	3·812	3·605	3·416	3·242	3·083	2·937	2·802
7·325	6·733	6·210	5·747	5·335	4·968	4·639	4·344	4·078	3·837	3·619	3·421	3·241	3·076	2·925
8·162	7·435	6·802	6·247	5·759	5·328	4·946	4·607	4·303	4·031	3·786	3·565	3·366	3·184	3·019
8·983	8·111	7·360	6·710	6·145	5·650	5·216	4·833	4·494	4·192	3·923	3·682	3·465	3·269	3·091
9·787	8·760	7·887	7·139	6·495	5·938	5·453	5·029	4·656	4·327	4·035	3·776	3·544	3·335	3·147
10·57	9·385	8·384	7·536	6·814	6·194	5·660	5·197	4·793	4·439	4·127	3·851	3·606	3·387	3·190
11·35	9·986	8·853	7·904	7·103	6·424	5·842	5·342	4·910	4·533	4·203	3·912	3·656	3·427	3·223
12·11	10·56	9·295	8·244	7·367	6·628	6·002	5·468	5·008	4·611	4·265	3·962	3·695	3·459	3·249
12·85	11·12	9·712	8·559	7·606	6·811	6·142	5·575	5·092	4·675	4·315	4·001	3·726	3·483	3·268
13·58	11·65	10·11	8·851	7·824	6·974	6·265	5·669	5·162	4·730	4·357	4·033	3·751	3·503	3·283
14·29	12·17	10·48	9·122	8·022	7·120	6·373	5·749	5·222	4·775	4·391	4·059	3·771	3·518	3·295
14·99	12·66	10·83	9·372	8·201	7·250	6·467	5·818	5·273	4·812	4·419	4·080	3·786	3·529	3·304
15·68	13·13	11·16	9·604	8·365	7·366	6·550	5·877	5·316	4·844	4·442	4·097	3·799	3·539	3·311
16·35	13·59	11·47	9·818	8·514	7·470	6·623	5·929	5·353	4·870	4·460	4·110	3·808	3·546	3·316
17·01	14·03	11·76	10·02	8·649	7·562	6·687	5·973	5·384	4·891	4·476	4·121	3·816	3·551	3·320
17·66	14·45	12·04	10·20	8·772	7·645	6·743	6·011	5·410	4·909	4·488	4·130	3·822	3·556	3·323
18·29	14·86	12·30	10·37	8·883	7·718	6·792	6·044	5·432	4·925	4·499	4·137	3·827	3·560	3·325
18·91	15·25	12·55	10·53	8·985	7·784	6·835	6·073	5·451	4·937	4·507	4·143	3·831	3·562	3·327
19·52	15·62	12·78	10·67	9·077	7·843	6·873	6·097	5·467	4·948	4·514	4·147	3·834	3·564	3·329
22·40	17·29	13·76	11·26	9·427	8·055	7·003	6·177	5·517	4·979	4·534	4·160	3·842	3·569	3·332
25·00	18·66	14·50	11·65	9·644	8·176	7·070	6·215	5·539	4·992	4·541	4·164	3·845	3·571	3·332
27·36	19·79	15·05	11·92	9·779	8·244	7·105	6·234	5·548	4·997	4·544	4·166	3·846	3·571	3·333
29·49	20·72	15·46	12·11	9·863	8·783	7·123	6·242	5·552	4·999	4·545	4·166	3·846	3·571	3·333
31·42	21·48	15·76	12·23	9·915	8·305	7·133	6·246	5·554	4·999	4·545	4·167	3·846	3·571	3·333

Index